Manor Publishing

Copyright © Stuart Finlay 2008.

This paperback edition first published in 2008 by Manor Publishing

Printing and binding locally sourced around the world.

A CIP catalogue record for this book is available from the British Library

E-Mail: enquiries@manorpublishing.com

ISBN-13: 978-0-9558178-0-9

I0472912

Dedication

To Sir Winston Churchill for writing such a wonderfully entertaining set of memoirs of the Second World War that inspired this book.

To Ruby my principal proof reader for your dedication and support.

To Fiona, my editor, for candidly helping me turn my ramblings into something readable.

To anyone who is about to read the book. I hope you enjoy it. Please do not take it too seriously or literally. Any opinions or historical overviews are entirely my own summations based on Churchill's and Roy Jenkins' books. I reserve the right to be wrong and to misinterpret every day.

To any serious Churchill historians please accept this as an exercise in capturing all that was positive about Churchill's management of the war, based on his memoirs. It does not take account of his record before or after the war. I appreciate that Churchill had his detractors. This book is by someone who has fallen under his spell and can only see the good that he did.

Contents

Preface

Another Book about Churchill?

A general who served under Sir Winston Churchill throughout the war famously stated that he was an exasperating task master, however, it was a privilege to serve under someone whose like existed on the earth only once every thousand years. It has to be possible to learn from a man whose existence is so rare.

The most accurate definition of this text would be an historical business improvement book that sets out in equal measure to entertain; to inform the reader about Churchill and derive some excellent business advice from one of the greatest Briton's that ever lived.

In the book, I take the golden nuggets of advice that Churchill gives to the reader of his WWII memoirs and referencing them against my own extensive business experience convert the advice into practical modern suggestion to help the reader improve their business performance. To avoid the book being another "dry as dust" business book I have filled each chapter with fascinating and unusual stories from the war.

When Churchill became Prime Minister in 1940, he famously stated that he felt as if he had been walking with destiny and all his past life had been but a preparation for the hour and the trial that was to come. He was 65 and had an amazingly jam-packed lifetime of experience. Given that most professional political leaders these days have little real world knowledge, I can think of no current politician that has one tenth of the life experience that Churchill amassed. These days he would be considered too old to be taken seriously. Thankfully, this was not the case in 1940.

I came upon Churchill's memoirs by pure chance after listening to Simon Scharma's History of Britain (on my IPOD), this led me to download Churchill's History of the English speaking peoples, volume 1. He wrote these books just before the war; however, the publishers delayed their release until after he completed his memoirs in the late 50's. The references to his war memoirs fascinated me and whilst stopping by chance at a second hand book warehouse I purchased all six original volumes for £25/$50.

The memoirs run to over four thousand pages of tiny print, the equivalent today of about six thousand pages. Whilst reading them it became clear just how brilliant Churchill was at orchestrating the people and events that led to victory in WWII. To my mind, these skills are relevant within the modern business world and echo throughout the decades.

This leaves two choices, purchase Churchill's memoirs, and digest the 6000 pages, (this should keep even the most proficient reader occupied for some time). Alternatively, trust that having read them twice, I have captured sufficient information to make this book a worthwhile investment.

It is unlikely that anyone will ever again have to orchestrate the defeat of a Nazi tyrant. The way Winston Churchill managed this task in conjunction with the USA and the rest of the allies is quite incredible. Reading his memoirs has really changed many of my preconceived ideas about Churchill and the events of WWII.

The memoirs show in detail how good he was as a manager of people, a negotiator and persuader and how the techniques he used consistently throughout the war, helped him keep on top of a myriad of simultaneous events across the globe.

This is not an analytical academic study of Churchill's memoirs. I have been a successful manager for many years in a number of large PLC's. I am not a CEO writing about how to make millions. I have been with my present company for five years and I have a good income; I am by modern definition a middle manager. The perspective of this book is entirely my own point of view, based on my real life experiences of business.

Churchill did not acquire his skills and techniques by reading management self-help books or going to seminars given by self-development gurus. To my knowledge, he had never been on a training course or learned how to develop the innumerable habits of an effective manager. Churchill never had a proper job in the conventional sense. He qualified for a commission in the army when he left school. He went to India and South Africa as a sub-lieutenant after graduating at Sandhurst Military College, adding to his income by writing articles for London newspapers. He then became a member of parliament. He gained his ability to motivate people and to manage the events of WWII so effectively through years of practice. By the time he became prime minister in 1940, he was sixty-five. Most people of this age would be looking forward to a happy life of retirement, not taking on the greatest single challenge to befall a man in recent history.

For many years, Churchill's only income came from writing books, newspaper articles and lecture tours. In spite of his privileged background, he actually had no money. In the pre-war years, he always tried to maintain his income within hailing distance of his outgoings. He was a great believer in trying to make reading an interesting and rewarding experience. His war memoirs span six books and apart from the appendixes are an incredibly interesting read. Some of the chapters in the second volume "Their Finest Hour" dealing with the fall of France and the Battle of Britain are just electrifying especially to someone British. Re-reading them on a long plane journey recently having had some pre-dinner wine, I had to wipe a tear of national pride from my eye.

This book is intended to be an entertaining and rewarding read both in terms of the lessons that can be learnt from Churchill (and there are many) as well as an interesting book in it's own right. I will share some of the background to the many big decisions and point out certain stories and events, which came as a surprise to me.

This text will be of most appealing to those who have an interest in Churchill or WWII and are active in business. The examples target the full gamut of working people from students and those setting out on a business career, to the more experienced. I hope that everyone reading this will take something away.

Each chapter of the book stands alone with some of the same events used throughout the book and examined from different angles. No promise is given that anyone reading this book will become an overnight success or radically change the way they work. In each of the chapters, I have used events and stories from 27 years of my own working life as examples to try and illustrate a particular point. Some of the chapters might resonate with the personal experiences of the reader. It would be disappointing if no chapter struck a chord. I hope that a business situation will arise were the reader will stop and think, what would Churchill do in this situation?

Incidentally, the name for the book actually came from just such an occasion; originally, I was going to call it, "If Churchill were in Business Today". Whilst attending a management training course the instructor suggested that when faced with an intractable problem, one way to break through a mental log jam is to put oneself in the position of a famous historical figure and ask what would they do, faced with the same situation. He then used the phrase "What Would Churchill Do".

Preface

Keep it Real

There have been hundreds of books written about achieving success in business. Some of them have been interesting to a greater or lesser extent. However, many endeavor to teach artificial techniques as a replacement for the basics.

The basic principle for any good business professional is to demonstrate integrity, honesty and trust whilst at the same time being completely candid and firm with people when necessary. By adding to that foundation any necessary skills needed for a specific type of business, covering all sorts of learned techniques or acquired talents, a successful future beckons.

Avoid substituting learned techniques for the basic principles, as colleagues and customers can quickly spot a fake. Layer the techniques onto the basic principles and you not only have a talented individual but someone who people will want to work with and with whom customers will want to do business.

Churchill received the love and respect of his people and was an incredibly effective manager of the war business at the same time. He commanded genuine loyalty from those around him, whilst acting in a ruthless fashion for the common good. When he gave progress updates to parliament he never shirked from delivering bad news, however he always managed to put the bad news into a context that at the very least made it understandable, if not necessarily palatable.

When the difficult decisions were left for Churchill alone to make he did not shy away from them; some of these decisions involved the loss of thousands of lives and were a direct result of his orders. In the end, he had the common good of the country and the defeat of the Nazi's as his main goal.

Churchill would support any country, which could help with the defeat of Germany, no matter how good or bad their regime was. It was by holding on to the principles of decency and firmness in his dealings that allowed him to do so.

Churchill understood the value of being perceived as a decent, trustworthy and honorable person. Without this, he would not have been able to carry Britain with him through the war. It is as true for business people today as it was for Churchill. Your most valuable asset is the way you are perceived in business.

Chapter 1

The Unintended Consequences of Treating People Decently

Churchill was a very demanding boss, driving his staff to the absolute limit of human endurance. Given the life and death nature of the circumstances, it is understandable why they would give their all to the task. He was however demonstrably fair and was always courteous in his dealings with staff. He could have quite understandably acted like a tyrant bullying people to do his bidding.

Churchill's management style of being demanding whilst at the same time being pleasant and courteous meant that the people he came into contact with not only gave their all, but did so willingly. On numerous occasions, he took time to send messages of thanks or congratulations to those who worked hard and achieved success. He did not give the appearance of taking things for granted.

His sense of decency and fair play, the hallmark of the western allies was to prove invaluable when the war was at its peak in March 1945. The allies were driving the Germans across the Rhine making rapid progress into Germany. Whilst the victories were difficult, progress was remarkably good.

Russian progress on the Eastern front was not as good. Whilst the Red Army was making advances, the Germans appeared to be fighting much harder for every mile of ground.

At this time, a row broke out between Russia, the USA and Great

Britain. This was the first major disagreement between the three powers, with the Soviets accusing the Allies of bad faith. During March 1945, a German general had made contact with the allies to explore potential terms of surrender, hoping to end the war in the North of Italy. The allies, uncertain if this was a genuine offer, arranged a meeting with the German General and a couple of SS officers in Switzerland. For logistical reasons the Soviets could not attend. At the meeting, the allies stated their position that only an unconditional surrender would be acceptable, with all troops required to become prisoners of War. This was important, as it was pointless if the Germans surrendered on one battlefront, only to transfer their troops to another.

Because the Soviets were not at the meeting, they became suspicious of the allies, assuming that Britain and the USA had struck some sort of deal, resulting in the German army fighting harder against the Soviets than the allies. The tone of the telegrams sent by Roosevelt and Churchill to Stalin protesting the innocence of the allies was brutal. This was all happening at the same time as the Soviets were effectively trying to annex Poland (later chapter). In the end, the allies just about managed to convince Stalin of their innocence, and the issue blew over.

By March 1945, the German army with the exception of Hitler and his immediate circle knew that they were going to lose the war, it was just a matter of time. The Battle of the Bulge was Hitler's last big push and he narrowly lost because of a lack of fuel.

Imagine you are a German soldier or officer struggling against the tough, hard fighting, Allied troops and have to surrender. Ending up as a prisoner of war, treatment was according to the Geneva Convention; there would be a good chance of seeing family and country again. The Red Army on the other hand had a reputation of being decidedly brutal towards captured prisoners, executing officers and shipping soldiers to far away frozen parts of Russia to be slave workers, never to return. The Soviet army also had a terrible reputation for the way in which they treated any population that they liberated.

In fairness to the Russians, the Germans did it to them. Hitler had instructed his Generals to treat the Russians with greater severity than the British, as they had not signed the Hague Convention on the treatment of prisoners.

The allies treated any population they liberated or soldiers they captured with decency and respect. The Soviets did the opposite, German soldiers were treated very badly and they were brutal towards the population of the countries they occupied. The German soldiers fought the Soviets so much harder for every mile of ground knowing that defeat or capture would lead to a bleak future. The evidence was plentiful given the way Russia had treated Poland. Germans knew that land captured by the Soviets would end up as part of a communist regime. Allied occupied land would eventually end up as a democratic state. Given the choice at the time no one would have wanted to be under communist rule, communism forced itself upon those countries occupied by the Soviets.

By continuing the policy of treating people harshly, the Soviets made it difficult for themselves. Stalin assumed that the allies had concluded a deal with the Germans, which wasn't correct. He simply failed to understand the difference his brutal policy had on the German army compared to that of the allies. For the sake of themselves and their country, a soldier preferred to be captured by the allies than the Soviets.

On a much smaller scale, the Red Army effect regularly applies in business situations. Over the years, I have worked with colleagues who complain that no one in internal departments ever does them any favors or helps them out. Such colleagues will often interact well with their peers and with customers, however staff within the supporting business departments find them difficult to work with.

In a sales role at a previous company, one of my team was a great example of this, for the purposes of this narrative, I will call him Martin. Martin and I had the same role selling for a young successful telecoms company. This involved plenty of interaction with different internal departments whilst in the office and on the road. Quickly resolving internal issues delivered better service to customers, brought in more business and put more money in my pocket.

If I visited an internal department shortly after Martin had been there and they realized I was in his team, the staff would be incredibly hostile towards me. It would be difficult to receive any assistance and I would have to work hard to demonstrate that not everyone treated people in the same way as Martin.

He took the approach with internal support staff that "I'm really important and you're not, so you had better complete this request and treat it like it is your number one priority", he would never say please or thank you. No pleasantries, no trying to understand the person's current workload, or how time consuming his request might be, just "do this because I want you to". He would then complain to anyone who would listen that so and so in the billing department was useless and never did anything for him.

Martin was consistent; he behaved like this with all internal departments. His behavior didn't lead to him losing his job, he was actually very good with customers but he didn't attain the success that others had. His approach cost him the difference between doing really well and doing okay. Internal staff would eventually do what he asked, assuming that it was a valid request, but begrudgingly and with the least amount of effort they could get away with.

Thankfully, once staff in the internal departments had worked with me I didn't have to contend with the same issues as Martin. I am no saint, however, I discovered early in my career that showing respect for a persons role and dealing with them in a reasonable manner whilst taking a few extra seconds to be pleasant makes such a difference to how willing they are to help. In effect, I treated internal staff as if they were customers. Martin just didn't appreciate that good internal relationships can make the difference between being successful and doing okay.

By taking a little extra time to explain why a request needs urgent attention and the difference some help could make, it is amazing how much easier it is to have something prioritized. People like to feel they have contributed; it is just basic human nature. When someone has done an exceptional job, take the time to say that you really appreciated their help.

Adopting this approach helps to become more effective and efficient, with less effort. Often, even when favors are not required, requests seem to speed through the system and the Martins of this world find their work requirements taking the longest time possible. People treated decently spread the word to other parts of the business. One simple act of being pleasant when making a request can make things easier when help is required from other parts of the company. The opposite is also true, take a Red Army approach and resistance can spring up in areas where it is least expected.

Russia could have made it much easier for German soldiers to stop fighting and surrender simply by changing their tactics and treating them decently. This would have prevented the loss of countless Soviet and German lives and enabled the Red army to occupy a larger part of Western Europe than they eventually did, helping them to carve up even more of Europe for their own benefit.

At the end of the war, German soldiers and civilians would travel hundreds of miles to surrender to the allies rather than risk the consequences of surrender to the Red Army. If you were a German scientist or highly skilled engineer, who would you prefer to work for, the brutal Soviets or the decent allies, a communist dictatorship or a democratic society? The allies gained enormous advantage and saved thousands of soldier's lives by behaving decently. They knew that by behaving this way they would have an advantage over the Soviets and gained enormously from the unintended consequences of doing so.

Taking the time to treat people well both in business and in all situations can make the difference between doing well and achieving great success.

Chapter 2

Don't Hesitate to be Pleasantly Ruthless

Churchill over the course of his life had developed the capability to be absolutely ruthless. He was quite comfortable giving bad news without losing any sleep over it. He was able to do this because he firmly believed that he was acting for the common good.

By Ruthless, I mean absolutely life and death ruthless.

It was May 1940 and Churchill had not long taken over as Prime Minister. He put all his efforts into persuading the French to keep fighting the Germans. Times were tough and a large part of the world was not convinced that Britain would survive. The British army had 400,000 troops fully equipped in France trying to resist the German invasion. Everything went horribly wrong, the Germans smashed through Belgium and the French army collapsed. The only question then was if the British army could get out of France intact.

The end of May brought incredible scenes of heroism; hundreds of small boats evacuated 350,000 troops from Dunkirk. They ferried backward and forward repeatedly across the channel, despite the peril of air attack and shelling from the shores of France small fishing boats and pleasure cruisers joined with the Royal Navy to bring relief to a desperate situation. Churchill was convinced that Hitler could quite easily have instructed his troops to obliterate the British army had he wished to. One theory put forward to explain why Hitler did not give the order was his absolute confidence in victory over Britain and a subsequent negotiated surrender. He wanted those soldiers to be able to police the Empire once Britain had capitulated. Thankfully, things panned out somewhat differently for Adolf.

Not long after Dunkirk the French army was defeated, the Vichy government was created as a puppet for the Germans. The overriding issue for the British was the future of the French Navy. France had the fourth biggest fleet in the world, and had state of the art battleships near completion in French dockyards.

The man in charge of the Fleet was Admiral Darlan. Darlan had given repeated assurances to Churchill that should France be defeated he would give the command to sail the fleet to Britain rather than see it fall into German hands. Had he stayed true to his word, Darlan would have been acclaimed in France and Britain as a hero. He might have ended up as popular as De-Gaulle, who fled France to set up a French opposition in Britain.

In what Churchill describes as an astonishing act of treachery Darlan reneged on his personal commitment and failed to give the command. According to Churchill, this was because Darlan had a new ministerial job in the Vichy government and it no longer served his personal interests to give the order.

Throughout Churchill's memoirs, he is scathing about certain historical figures but he saves some of his most derisory comments for Darlan, calling him an arrogant self-seeking publicist who threw away the chance to be a great savior of France. Instead, he suffered a miserable existence for a few years under the yoke of German control, only to die, assassinated by his own people. To his credit he never let the Germans get access to the French fleet.

After the miraculous evacuation from Dunkirk, the British were desperately short of guns and ammunition given that most of it languished in France. Churchill asked Roosevelt to sell Britain fifty old American destroyers to help protect the vital convoys crossing the Atlantic. He also asked to buy a million rifles to re-equip the army. The Americans were hesitant to supply the weapons, as they were not convinced that Britain could survive. It was one thing for Churchill to state in a famous speech that Britain would fight the Germans on the beaches and in the countryside. It was quite another for America to supply vast arms to Britain believing that the Germans would be pointing them back at the USA at some time in the near future.

The issue of the French Navy, the perception of Britain and Churchill's will to fight were resolved simultaneously. By dealing with the French Navy in a ruthless manner, Churchill sent an unequivocal message to the world that Britain intended to fight on, no matter what the cost, and had ruled out any thoughts of a negotiated surrender.

Churchill gave the Vichy government three options, hand the ships to the British, scuttle them, or sail them out of harms way to the Caribbean or Canada. One thing was certain he was not going to allow them to fall into German hands.

General Weygand, the French Prime Minister, was informed by Darlan that Britain had given the French Navy only two options, he deliberately omitted option three, sailing the ships to the Caribbean. Churchill was acting ruthlessly for the common good however; option three showed that he was also being reasonable and sensitive to French feelings. Had Weygand known about option three he would have ordered Darlan to accept.

Taking option three was not in Darlan's interests; this would have spread his power base across the world and out of his control. Darlan's treacherous decision to conceal option three ultimately led to 1500 French sailors being killed.

To ensure that the French did not try to make a run for it, the British fleet was mobilized and squadrons dispatched to intercept the two main groups of French ships. One of the British Admirals managed to persuade his opposite number to surrender his ships to the British. The other battle group guarding a large fleet of French ships moored at Oran was not so successful. In essence, there was a standoff. The British Admirals repeated attempts to come to an agreement failed. Churchill was not going to flinch, unlike the previous Prime Minister Chamberlain; he gave the order to attack the French ships if they failed to heed a final warning.

The British Admiral passed on the ultimatum to the French, who decided to make a run for it and opened fire on the British Navy. They in turn, launched a counter attack and sank or disabled all the French ships, whilst suffering some minor damage themselves. Fifteen hundred French sailors perished despite the best efforts of the British to save as many lives as possible. If Darlan had done the right thing, the Oran incident would never have happened.

The sinking of the French ships at Oran sent a message around the world that Britain was deadly serious about fighting to the bitter end and would stop at nothing in the best interests of preserving her freedom. Shortly afterwards the guns arrived from America, a few months later the destroyers sailed across the Atlantic to be put into the service of the British Navy. The deal for the destroyers was long before lend lease and involved Britain giving ninety nine year leases for air bases in Bermuda and parts of the Caribbean. After Oran, no one was in any doubt about Britain's resolve to survive. The next big test, the Battle of Britain was to follow.

Whilst the Oran incident showed Churchill's ruthless streak it also demonstrated how he went out of his way to act decently towards the French Navy. He insisted on giving plenty of warning to the French, he was desperate to avoid any loss of life. The British Navy did not try to surprise the French or do anything underhand. They tried and tried to come to a settlement. In the end, it just was not acceptable to see the Germans take control of the ships as this could have destabilized the whole balance of naval superiority that Britain enjoyed over them, the one area in which Britain had the upper hand.

Churchill acted both decently and ruthlessly, something he was to do many times during the course of the war. He stated that his decision to sink the ships of a country that Britain had been allies with, only weeks before, was the most difficult he ever had to take. Whilst he did not regret it, he wished that it had been avoidable.

Sadly, had option three been given to the French the Oran disaster could easily have been averted.

Churchill knew that by establishing his credentials as a person of stern resolve, if he said he was going to do something or issued an ultimatum then all the governments and people he dealt with would know the consequences should they fail to act. His capacity to deliver on any threats or ultimatums was no longer in any doubt.

Another example of Churchill's pleasant ruthlessness came after Pearl Harbor. The end of the declaration of war that Britain made on Japan read, "His Majesty's ambassador in Tokyo has been instructed to inform the Imperial Japanese Government in the name of His Majesty's Government that a state of war exists between our two countries. I have the honor to be with high consideration, sir, your obedient servant, Winston S Churchill." Churchill was criticized for the pleasant way he ended the letter. As Churchill put it, "when you have to kill a man it costs nothing to be polite".

It is highly desirable to create the business perception of somebody who will carry out a threat or an ultimatum. When a person will do what they say, when they say it, even if it means there will be unpleasant consequences, they are instinctively treated differently. If they can achieve this whilst demonstrating integrity, being pleasant and avoiding obvious confrontation, they retain respect, even when the outcome is unpalatable. Genuine respect is one of the hardest things to achieve in business.

Its one thing to manage by dictation, bullying and fear. It is something entirely different to be ruthless, respected and admired at the same time. I would contend that Churchill had the latter in abundance and it was a factor of his success.

My apologies in advance for using an example from my own career, which pales in comparison to Churchill. It is not necessary to be in a life and death situation or to do anything overly dramatic for colleagues or staff to know you are being serious. Being candid, I would probably be described as firm rather than ruthless.

I took on a management role with a new company and started in the summer. In the process, I inherited a team of three people. When December came all of my team vanished for most of the month, they had holiday days left over and wanted to take them before the calendar year end cut-off.

It seemed odd that everyone would leave it so late in the year to take such a large amount of holiday. On investigation, I discovered that company policy was to allocate all fixed public holidays as floating days; staff could either work them or take them off. My team all worked from home as they lived a long distance from the nearest office. They claimed to be working the public holidays from their home office when the rest of the country was also on holiday. In reality, they kept their mobile phone on just in case of emergency. By doing this, they accrued additional holiday. They would take five weeks annual leave during the year, then indignantly insist on taking their accrued floating days in December.

It would have been easy and personally beneficial to turn a blind eye, especially considering the rest of the company were largely relaxed about it. Other managers in the company were happy to take advantage. I remember chatting to one manager who had the ludicrous situation of a salesperson taking the week before Christmas and the week after as holiday, insisting that she would work from home on the three quiet days between Christmas and New Year. What a likely story!

This extra holiday made my team less effective. I was launching a brand new business and it was imperative that they put in maximum effort, not easy if they were on leave. I solved the problem by issuing a new holiday directive, this allowed everyone to continue working public holidays, so long as they did so from a company office. No one ever worked them again as it would have meant at least a one hundred mile round trip.

An option to carry up to five days of annual leave across to the following year was commonplace and was at the discretion of the manager. This just encouraged people not to take them, resulting in greater stress, whilst stopping them spending time with their families. I stopped the carry over and insisted that only one week of holiday could be taken in December. The rules applied to everyone without exception, including myself. From then on, the team took their holidays during the year and in my view were more productive and happier as a result.

Whilst these examples were very low level, they demonstrated a principled approach and a certain amount of resolve. Nobody liked the new rules, however boundaries had been set which began the process of the team developing respect for me as a manager.

Building on the theme of developing respect, I was in the office sitting near the support team when they overheard me having a conversation with a project manager who had just given me some bad news regarding the delivery of a service I was working on. This caused a robust argument over the phone. After the phone call they all looked at each other and said, we had better not mess with that guy; he bites your head off. Whilst I wasn't rude to the project manager I made it clear that the revised proposal was unacceptable and offered advice as to how to make improvements.

It only takes a simple incident like the one described for people to understand that you can be ruthless and firm when called for. It is unnecessary to be ruthless all the time, as people will understand that certain boundaries exist that would be unwise to cross. Within the boundaries, it is possible to act in an entirely pleasant manner.

Ruthlessness, respect and admiration are probably the hardest things to achieve in business, however to be successful these qualities are not required. There are plenty of examples of truly dreadful people, who have been successful because they were bullies and treated staff appallingly. In my industry, I know plenty of very wealthy people that fall into both categories.

Of the successful and demonstrably great people, one person stands out as the sort of successful businessperson I would like to emulate. He is just the nicest person you could hope to meet, he is very wealthy and could sell up his business and retire any time he liked. He is well known in the UK Telecoms industry, I have never met anyone who did not like him. Having strived hard for his success, his rewards are justly deserved. He has been able to combine great business acumen and a ruthless instinct for the right product or service. Most of his employees have worked for him for many years and cannot speak highly enough of him. There simply are not enough people like him in the business world.

Given the option of achieving success like the person described above, or doing so whilst thoroughly loathed by everyone, I know which I prefer. Based on the people I have met, it would appear possible to choose which option to take.

Chapter 3

Stop & Smell the Roses

Churchill's memoirs clearly described how he took time to recharge his batteries whenever possible, despite being under almost incalculable pressure. He absolutely subscribed to the work hard play hard approach to life, at a level that most people today would struggle to match.

Churchill spent many months out of the country during the war and was even criticized by the press at home for taking too many trips abroad. These criticism's must have seemed very unfair to Churchill, as it would not have been possible for him to have such an extraordinary influence on the direction of the war, if he had stayed in Britain.

It was during these frequent trips to places such as North Africa, America, Canada and Russia that he endeavored to travel in the greatest degree of comfort possible, taking time to enjoy the journey. Whilst negotiating or persuading he would ensure the best use was made of any hospitality on offer. At the end of his trips, he would plan additional time to recuperate and recharge his batteries.

Churchill's idea of relaxing wasn't like most mortals. He would go to bed very late, sleep for eight hours then lay in until early afternoon reading and responding to a mountain of telegrams, part of the unrelenting, decision making process of war. He always travelled with an entourage of secretaries who he dictated to, along with an encryption team responsible for securely transmitting his messages around the world.

Churchill was regularly ill during the war being particularly prone to colds and flu; this meant he was often laid up in bed. Even when he was desperately ill and barely able to walk, he would still attend a conference. His personal doctor worked wonders to keep him fit during the war.

One of his favorite locations was Marrakech; he loved to stay in the opulence of the American ambassador's house, which had fantastic views over the Atlas Mountains. In fact, he produced his only painting during the war on one such visit. Churchill was a prolific painter using painting as means of relaxation. He even managed to publish a book about painting after the war.

Given the pressures upon him, it would have been completely understandable if Sir Winston had left no time for himself, devoting every single waking minute to the war effort. The impression given is that he was not a particularly religious man, believing that he would stride the earth once with little expectation of a hereafter. He therefore went to great lengths to enjoy the time available.

There is a great anecdote in his memoirs about an incident, which took place in early 1945, whilst Churchill was on his way back to Britain from a conference with Roosevelt and Stalin in Yalta, Russia. He made a stopover in Egypt to meet an important Arab Prince who had been very loyal to the war effort, providing the allies with oil. The Prince was on board an American battle ship, which had transported him along with his 10 wives, 60 servants and a dozen goats. Dinner was arranged by the Prince's personal assistant who wrote to Churchill informing him that because of the Prince's religion, no alcohol would be permitted during dinner. Churchill was famous for enjoying a drink with a reputation for preferring the finest wines, champagnes and cognacs. There was no possibility whatsoever that Churchill would abstain from a drink during dinner. He diplomatically wrote to the Prince and stated that, whilst respecting His Highness's convictions, abstinence during a meal would offend his own belief that he should be allowed to drink before during and after every meal. Dinner proceeded without incident!

For ordinary working people such as I, with a wife and two young boys, cramming lots of fun and excitement into life can be a challenge. After seventeen years of marriage, the only thing that will part Fiona and myself will be when one of us ends up in a wooden box. We never tire of each other's company. Spending time with the children is great fun, although they are now approaching that age when I have to compete with the attractions of an X-Box. Thankfully, my work is enjoyable, rewarding, pays well and provides plenty of opportunities to do and see different things. Work that enables me to spend time with my family and to stop and smell the roses occasionally is of the utmost importance to me but this has not always been the case.

Please forgive the negativity of the following few pages, they are intended to illustrate how really bad managers can have a massive impact on the business and private lives of their staff as a result of the stress they cause.

The job before last was terribly difficult, the kids were young my immediate manager was a decent person but the senior manager was dreadful, although even worse examples are detailed below.

The senior manager had without doubt one of the sharpest minds of any person I have ever worked for, along with absolutely no ability whatever to interface with other people. He had no thought for the lives of staff outside of work. Treating them as a commodity to be used without consideration. It was common to work fourteen hours a day, 5 days a week, only to put in half a day at the weekend. He would think nothing of making staff stay late even if they had plans. He subscribed to a blame culture which meant his team spent their time trying not to do anything wrong, rather than do something creative. Because he was so intellectually sharp, compared to the rest of his management team, he would concentrate on criticizing his team's work because he knew he had the upper hand intellectually. This constant negativity created great stress and anxiety in advance of the monthly meetings. I recall one time being hailed as a hero by my colleagues, for winning an argument with him during a management meeting, it was such a rarity.

Those who know me would not recognize the permanently stressed out person I was then. One day during a moment of clarity amid the chaos, it dawned on me that life was too short to keep burning myself out and that another job was required. I have never looked back since and it is only right to say a big thank you to my old director. Working for him prepared me for working with almost anyone.

But life has a habit every now and then of dealing out poetic justice. Shortly after my departure, he moved roles within my old company and started working for a Frenchman, who was so difficult to work for he made my old senior manager look like a saint. To this day I have never heard anyone say a good word about the Frenchman. Although to be fair, women loved his Charles Aznavour French accent, staring dreamily at him during presentations.

He had what appeared to be a real hatred for any other human being. When he became MD of Europe, he continued to make my old directors life hell bullying him and slowly stripping him of his dignity, poetic justice! The Frenchman was fired as MD of Europe, the result of a failed business strategy.

He immediately re-surfaced in the telecoms industry. This coincided with my own move into telecoms. A few years later I was at an event and I overheard someone who had recently finished working for him describing how awful he was. He re-told a great story that really got to the nub of why everyone loathed him. A senior telecoms director who worked for the Frenchman booked an annual holiday in the Italian lakes. Months later a board meeting was called, which coincided with the director's family holiday. The Frenchman insisted that he came back from Italy to attend the meeting.

The meeting started to run late so the director stood up and made his excuses, explaining that he had to get back to the airport or he would miss his flight. The Frenchman angrily shouted at him in front of the other directors, "how dare you leave the meeting before it is finished", arrogantly stating "you will just have to get another flight tomorrow", accusing him of being disloyal and not committed to the company. All the other directors at the meeting knew that it served no purpose for him to remain, it was just one example of the way the Frenchman treated people by bullying them and belittling them in front of their peers. Incidentally, if at this point you sympathize with the Frenchman then this book is probably not for you!

The Frenchman eventually "left" the telecoms company, went to another business, then "left" there also three months later and not from choice. This same man once threatened a friend of mine that he would immediately sack any of the product marketing team who gave a bad presentation at a press launch.

For the last ten years, I have been very lucky, I have only had one brief stint working for a man who was completely unsuited for his role and managed to gain the sort of respect you reserve for a neighbors vicious dog. You do not like it, you cannot do anything about it, and you want it to go away, but ultimately it could hurt you if you mess with it. Shortly after he took over as the head of my division, I decided it was time to move on.

Whilst he was just trying to put food on the table for his family, in the best way he knew how, I believe he had a hole in his bucket. Whilst difficult to explain without sounding stupid, I like this analogy. Assume that everyone carries inside them a bucket of goodness. Unless a person's bucket is full, they feel out of balance and need to take action to fill it. A decent person will do something good, which will fill their bucket. A bad person, will top up the bucket, by doing something bad, to someone decent.

In the cases of the three people described, for one reason or another, known only to them, they have big holes in their respective buckets. They needed to treat people badly in order to fill their buckets up and feel good about themselves.

From a productivity perspective acting like a bully can create a short-term improvement in productivity, in the long term it tends to be counterproductive. Often cited as the catalyst of a blame culture, leading to people doing what they have to do, whilst avoiding taking any risks for fear of getting into trouble.

Churchill would regularly visit the war zones to get a feel for troop morale. If he sensed that it was low, he would ascertain why. If he concluded that poor leadership was the cause, he would quickly make changes. Above all, he knew only too well that motivated troops can make the difference between winning and losing a battle.

Quick comic anecdote about a lady who once worked for me. Not long after she started we went on some customer appointments. In the first client's office I noticed that she had brought a laptop computer in with her, I asked why and she said that her previous manager had insisted she take one into every customer meeting. I asked if she was planning to use the laptop and she said no, I thought this a bit odd but ignored it. Then she pulled out a notebook and apologized for only having a ballpoint pen to write with. At this point I thought she had some sort of obsessive compulsive disorder. "Why apologize," I asked. It transpired that her previous manager insisted on the use of fountain pens. I had to do everything in my power not to fall about in fits of laughter.

After the meeting I asked if her old boss had any other rules. It transpired that he insisted women had to wear "power suits"; all the men had to wear hand tailored "Saville Row" type suits along with expensive shirts, cufflinks and handmade leather shoes. He issued all new staff with a page of dress instructions. He disciplined anyone who did not adhere to his code. I was astonished that he could not trust well-paid salespeople to dress themselves.

I made it clear that I trusted my team to dress appropriately. We would regularly joke about the conversation, without thinking of the reason behind it. Later on she realized that enforcing the excessive dress code was one part of his controlling behavior which among other things made her feel bullied, and caused her to leave.

Stopping to smell the roses requires time to be set aside even from the busiest schedule. When a job is so consistently demanding that it leaves no time to enjoy life, then that job should be re-evaluated. Notwithstanding financial and family commitments it could be better to move on and work somewhere else, or be self-employed, than resent going to work every day. Thankfully, I have always managed to move from those businesses where I worked for bullies, although I did not think of it in those terms at the time. I was just unhappy. It is only with hindsight that I now realize that bullying was the cause of all the stress and anxiety. I just assumed that permanent aggravation was the norm when you worked for a big organization; it often is, but it does not have to be .Although I moved on more by luck than planning, looking back, I wish I had done so sooner.

Times are different, we all live in an age when phones and messaging devices keep us in constant contact with the office, creating the opportunity to work all hours of the day and night. It is sad when someone out for a family dinner cannot resist the temptation to respond to a message from work when they hear a beep or feel a buzz. There is no opportunity to "switch off" which eventually leads to a resentment of the job. Amazingly even when on a family holiday they feel compelled to take their laptop "just in case", ending up sitting by a pool watching the kids splash about whilst being too busy to join in. Scared stiff, that even from thousands of miles away, work will fall apart without them.

Breaking the cycle is not easy, and can take considerable courage. Generally, a good manager will not try to contact a member of staff at weekends or while they are on holiday, as they understand that when staff get a clean break from work they perform better when they return. Other managers through incompetence or malice will take as much as someone is prepared to give, happily phoning and e-mailing staff at all hours expecting a quick response without any consideration for their personal circumstances. I am a stickler for not contacting members of my team out of hours, new members of staff are in no doubt that working late into the evening and at weekends is not expected. Far better that employees give everything to the job when they are supposed to, then get some down time, rather than be permanently connected to the umbilical cord of work, leading to reduced effectiveness.

In a previous job, one chap called me the day before going on a two-week holiday to give me his personal mobile phone number because the company mobile wouldn't work abroad. This was just in case any big issues cropped up whilst he was away. I made it abundantly clear that no matter what happened he would not be getting a call from me, I joked that I would sack him if he contacted the office or a colleague. I wanted him to have a real break from work, something less available in his previous job. I selfishly denied him the opportunity to feel indispensable whilst on vacation because I wanted a more efficient and committed team member to return.

Taking time out for personal enjoyment and relaxation, even on a small scale, must add to the number of years we are likely to reside on this planet. If Churchill could spend time during a war to experience everything around him, making the effort to rest and recuperate, it must be possible for 21st Century workers to attempt to do the same. After all Churchill lived until he was ninety!

Chapter 4

Your Past can be a Bridle or a Spur

Churchill used this phrase in his memoirs. In planning for the Normandy invasions, Churchill had on his mind the terrible events of WWI, when hundreds of thousands of lives had been lost making direct frontal attacks against the Germans. These thoughts sat heavily upon him while planning for D-Day June 1944.

In the Great War millions had died on the battlefields of the Somme and Passchendaele, bogged down in trenches in the most appalling conditions. Churchill had been a member of the Government in World War 1 and had firsthand experience of the horrors of war. How a well developed defense and the use of machine guns could pin down armies for weeks at a time and kill thousands of young men in a single assault, just to gain a few hundred yards of muddy field.

Imagine yourself in Churchill's situation; you have lived through the horrors of World War 1 and here you are about to do the same thing again in 1944. Given conventional wisdom you just would not do it, which is where the phrase "your past can be a bridle or a spur" is apt. Just to explain a bridle is strapped to a horses head and slows it down when pulled. You can spur a horse on to go faster by the use of a whip. I do not mean to be insulting but you never know who will be reading this.

Churchill explained that lessons from the past should not hinder doing something in the future, if plans have been made to avoid making the same mistake twice.

During my time at one company, I was asked to set up a new service similar to a business I ran in a previous job. All was going well and I expected to launch within 3-4 months from my start date.

Whilst driving home one Friday afternoon in October I received a phone call from my office (hands free I might add), the voice assumed that I knew who he was. I did not have a clue, but carried on as if I did, rather than cause offence. He quizzed me about the service I was launching with a rather negative tone, which was annoying. I remained quiet and attentive because he seemed as if he might be important. Certain characters just have the ability to convey their position without actually saying I'm so-and-so and I'm really powerful so don't mess with me. He made it clear he was unhappy about what I was doing and wanted to see my manager and myself as soon as possible.

I made a couple of calls trying to find out who on earth he was, they confirmed that he was indeed extremely important and could quite comfortably bury my project if he wanted to.

Not the best news to hear on a Friday afternoon, the next thing was a call to his personal assistant to set up a meeting with him ASAP.

The only slot available for the next two weeks was Monday, three days time! I was distressed at the prospect of spending the weekend creating a presentation to convince him I was doing the right thing for the business. Development budget had been allocated; everyone else who mattered in the business was completely comfortable with the project. Unfortunately, he could have snatched the rug from underneath me. The job was great, I was well paid and I wanted to keep the rug under my feet.

The conversation I had with my boss at the time has etched in my memory. "Cancel what you are doing on Monday," I said. "We have to go and present the business case for the project to the senior director who just phoned me. Incidentally, he's annoyed with you for not telling him about it in the first place". My boss's response was typical. "These people really wind me up, expecting us to drop everything and jump at their command, and anyway, why on earth would I have told him about the project, it's nothing to do with him". After further heated discussion, we arranged the flights.

On the Monday, we presented our case, and this is where we get to the punch line. He had looked after a similar type of business in another country and had issues with the fraudulent use of the service. Even though this was some years before and systems and security measures had much improved, he just would not countenance the idea of launching the same type of service in his company.

He had let his previous experience become a bridle, even after we had presented a compelling case, which addressed all the issues, he was adamant about not allowing the service to go ahead. He was not prepared to accept that I had incorporated the lessons of the past into the new plan.

If Churchill had taken this approach we might not have had the Normandy landings in the early hours of June 6, 1944 and whilst we would have gone on to win the war, the time it took may have been extended to Hitler's advantage, as will be seen later in the book.

What Churchill actually did was use the lessons from the past, to guide him in considering the issues that presented themselves in 1944. In WW1, air superiority did not count for much, as planes did not have powerful enough guns and could not carry enough bombs to really make a big impact on the ground. In WWII air superiority made a huge difference, in fact it formed the basis of the Allied victory.

Before the landings in France, Churchill made sure the German defenses were heavily targeted, making sure to bomb the locations where the allies would land, in equal measure with the places where they would not. In addition, and of equal importance, all bridges and railway lines leading to the beaches were destroyed, making it difficult for the Germans to send in fresh troops before the allies could safely establish themselves in France. Churchill ensured that the number of troops were considerably larger than the original numbers planned for the landings. He had a large number of specialized weapons developed to help overcome the considerable German beach defenses.

Designation of the landing zones had taken place long before D-Day; the British and Commonwealth troops had specific beaches allocated, with the Americans planning to attack others. The movie "Saving Private Ryan" gives some idea of the scale and nature of the difficulties facing the Americans at Omaha beach. Whilst the British had difficulties landing, they were not nearly as bad as the difficulties experienced by American forces at Omaha. Most of the landing beaches were manned by what Churchill described as low-grade forces. Unfortunately for the Americans shortly before D-Day the troops at Omaha were replaced by fresh well-prepared, first-rate German troops. Hence the reason behind the terrible loss of American life on Omaha beach in comparison with the other landing zones.

Watching war movies would give the impression that it was largely American troops taking part in D-Day. In fact when the landings took place the troops had a split of 65/35 British/American. This ratio had reversed within six months.

After Dunkirk, Churchill began considering the practicalities of a return to France. The planners assumed that it would be impossible to successfully capture a large port before it was destroyed by the Germans. They had to develop a method of landing the vast quantities of men and the millions of tons of equipment needed to wage war, onto a beach. Given tides and the swell from waves, it was not possible to do this conventionally. Churchill had already set up a team to look at ways of overcoming this major obstacle. By the time of the D Day landings, a giant floating harbor had been developed called a Mulberry. This was sunk off the beach and bolted together, thus enabling all the supplies to be landed safely.

The Germans had not expected the allies to land on the 6th June because the weather had been so poor beforehand; the forecast for the sixth was not considered good enough by the German forecasters. The allies however had little choice. Even though the weather wasn't perfect, they had hundreds of ships loaded with troops who had been kept on board for 3 days. No one was allowed to disembark in order to preserve secrecy. The decision, taken on balance, was to "go now", rather than wait another month and risk even worse weather. The rough landings caused some of the amphibious tanks to sink but the element of surprise achieved by the allies outweighed these losses.

Churchill was convinced that modern warfare would overcome the problems of the past. He was right. On D-Day, only three thousand men died and by the end of June, this figure was only eight thousand. Whilst this was a large number, it only represented a very small percentage of the men landed and was a far smaller number than most people would assume.

The point Churchill was trying to make when he used the phrase "your past can be a bridle or a spur" is that people should endeavor to take positive lessons from the mistakes of the past and not dismiss doing something just because it went badly the last time. By taking the time to discover why problems occurred and creating effective plans to avoid them in the future, anything is possible.

Regarding the launch of my new service, to overcome the concerns raised, the business agreed to put in additional security measures. Whilst it was a close run thing, the project got approval and with the issue settled, the senior director eventually became a helpful supporter.

Chapter 5

The Habit of Detail

At the very outbreak of the war, Prime Minister Chamberlain appointed Churchill head of the Admiralty, giving him complete charge of the Navy. He effectively got his old job back as he had been head of the Admiralty for a time during WW1. Churchill immediately sent a memo to everyone in his department stating that he would not take responsibility for any decision attributed to him, which was not in writing. He kept to this principle when he became Prime Minister and Minister of Defense in March 1940.

Churchill was a prolific writer of telegrams and ciphers, the wartime equivalent of E-Mail. He would continually dictate memo's to his secretaries, issuing instructions and asking questions of the people and departments that dealt with every aspect of making war. What set him apart from previous Prime Ministers was his habit of attending to detail. He wanted to know about everything and he looked closely at all areas, he did not leave anything to chance.

This created a workload that would have floored a man half his age. To keep up with such a prolific level of detail, Churchill would typically work 18 hours a day requiring secretaries to work around the clock, just to keep up with him. He managed to achieve this constant level of productivity by sleeping for an hour every day after lunch. He had picked up this habit when he was a young man on adventure in Cuba with the Spanish army.

Churchill was very explicit, no interruptions during his nap. In fact, he had a golden rule regarding sleep in general; if a German invasion force landed in England, wake him up otherwise he was not to be disturbed. Remarkably, the D Day landings started on the morning of June the 6th at 4.00am, Churchill found out about the successful landings at 7.00am when he woke up. Can you imagine these days sleeping through such a momentous event!

Having a nap in the early afternoon can really work for some people. I returned from holiday and was working from home, I woke up very early to catch up on my E-Mail. By lunchtime, I was flagging, the jet lag had kicked in and I could barely keep my eyes open. Rather than the usual trick of drinking lots of strong coffee and just pushing through the exhaustion I thought I would try a "Churchill" and go to bed for an hour. Instead of a lunch break, I ate a sandwich at my desk.

It took a little while to fall asleep, fifty minutes later the alarm went off. I had probably slept for thirty and felt a bit groggy when I woke up, ten minutes later I could not believe how fresh I felt. I was a new man full of energy and concentration and able to get through a stack more work, with far greater concentration than I had managed in the run up to lunch. I felt fantastic for the rest of the day and into the evening. I thought it might spoil my sleep at night, but this was not the case.

It would be great if I could have a "Churchill" every day but given the nature of my job, that is not practical. I would love to have an airline Club Class chair in my study at home; I could then have a lunchtime sleep when I felt the need, again not very realistic. Everyone's circumstances are different and it might not be possible to grab a sleep for most people. If there is any way of squeezing an hour's sleep into a schedule or taking a quick nap in the car, or just sitting in a chair with eyes closed for twenty minutes. It is surprising how the body responds to a quick pit stop.

I do wonder if the fact that Churchill took a nap every day added to his longevity? He died at the age of ninety; he had lived a life filled with the most incredibly stressful events; he smoked huge cigars and was famous for enjoying a drink. By any insurance company's estimate he should have been dead at fifty. It is not impossible to imagine that taking an hours sleep every day could make a big difference to a person's health and overall sense of calm and well-being. I am no doctor but you never know, it might be the secret to a healthier extended life.

Churchill's memoirs contain many examples of his requests for information about a myriad of things, which affected every aspect of the war, at home and abroad. He was fanatical about checking every detail; from the farming of vegetables to the building of bombers, no area was too small for him.

When Churchill took over at the admiralty he checked if the sailors at the large naval base in Portsmouth had enough warm coats, and if there was enough entertainment in Portsmouth to keep the sailors occupied during shore leave. Not the sort of thing someone in Churchill's position would normally take an interest in. By delving down into this level of detail, he put everyone below him on notice that he had the desire and the capacity to get involved to the tiniest degree. The consequence of this approach was to motivate the people who worked in the admiralty to show the same attention to detail. If they did not, then the chief could expose any shortcomings or the cutting of corners at any time.

The example of making sure the sailors were well looked after also highlights Churchill's appreciation that it is people at the top who make the policies and people at the shop front who turn policy into reality, or victory, in the case of war.

During a committee meeting discussing the effect of German bombing in 1944 it was mentioned by one of the officers that German bombs developed a 30% greater bomb blast per pound than British bombs. Churchill immediately demanded to know why this was the case. It transpired that the Germans added aluminum powder to their explosive mixture, which increased the effective blast. In 1940 aluminum was in short supply, all-available aluminum went into making fighters and bombers, British bomb producers had taken the decision not to use aluminum. This decision had remained unchallenged for four years, despite aluminum being in plentiful supply in 1944. This meant that Britain had to send more bombers to Germany to have the same impact as the Germans did when they sent bombers to Britain. The lack of attention to detail by the bomb manufacturers was limiting the effectiveness of British war making. Churchill immediately gave the instruction to build all new bombs with the revised explosive mixture, to the detriment of the German population.

Another example of attention to detail involved the diet of the troops. In 1940 essential food imports from around the world were decreasing as merchant ships were continually being sunk by U-Boats. Churchill created a scientific committee to investigate the nutrition of the troops and the wider population as a whole. They recommended the rationing of tea and that all troop meals consist of a high-energy diet of vegetables, nuts and pulses. Churchill immediately intervened and asked professor Lindeman (the scientist he trusted most of all) to evaluate the proposals. He concluded that rationing tea was one sure way of upsetting the working population. Churchill was not happy with the troop rationing proposals and stated that, "All the food faddists and nut eaters I have ever known died young after a long period of senile decay". He insisted that the troops received rations of meat and vegetables, as one sure way to lose the war was to upset the soldiers by putting them on a vegetarian diet. He insisted that tea remained in plentiful supply for as long as possible.

It is astonishing, that with the fall of France and the Battle of Britain to contend with, Churchill could find time to attend to such matters.

Another example of Sir Winston managing detail had a significant effect on the War and in particular made an enormous contribution to the turn around in the fortunes of the British army.

In the early part of the war, the British army had ejected the Italians from North Africa as part of the western desert campaign; these victories were the first real success the British army had achieved. This all changed when the German army arrived on the scene. They had superior equipment, were better organized and had in Rommell a formidable General. The Germans started to win back the Italian territory lost to the British; ending with what Churchill considered a humiliating defeat, when the heavily fortified port of Tobruk surrendered to a German force one third its size.

Churchill heard about the surrender whilst he was at a strategy and planning conference in Washington. President Roosevelt delivered the news to him personally. Churchill took the news very badly and resolved to make changes to the command structure in the western dessert, to enable the British army to fight more effectively.

Before he did this, he asked a big favor of Roosevelt. The US had just introduced the Sherman tank, which was widely regarded as the finest tank in the world at the time, far superior to the British tank. Churchill discovered that when the British tanks engaged the German Panzer tanks they were soundly beaten. Not surprisingly, in a tank battle, how good your tanks are is a crucial factor. The British tank was better than the Italian, but not as good as the German.

It transpires that whilst talking to my mother about this book I was told that my grandfather who was in the army engineering corp during the dessert campaign took it upon himself to design an additional steel plate for the British tank which helped saved countless lives by giving increased protection to the occupants when the tank was attacked.

If you are in an army and know that the opposition's tank is capable of destroying yours relatively easily, you fight with a massive physical handicap. It must also have a psychological effect when an army knows that they are effectively fighting with one hand tied behind their back.

The USA had started mass-producing Sherman's and the first 300 tanks were on their way to a division of rangers. Churchill asked that Roosevelt divert the tanks from the eager American troops and have them shipped across the ocean to North Africa.

He then went to Cairo where the command structure for the British army was based. Churchill altered it enabling senior commanders to be closer to the action enabling them to take responsibility for a smaller theatre of war.

It was at this time that one of Britain's most famous field marshals took the job of commanding the British Eighth army, nicknamed the Desert Rats, by a twist of fate. Churchill actually gave command of the Eighth army to General Gott but unfortunately, by sheer bad luck he died the next day, shot down flying into Cairo for a weekend break, the same route Churchill used the day before. Field Marshall Montgomery took on what must have seemed a daunting task the next day. He was actually working with Eisenhower in England on plans for the D Day invasion when the news came of Gott's premature death. He flew immediately to North Africa and started to shake things up.

Monty revised the tactics the Army used when engaging the German Panzers, in particular the use of field guns at close range to disable them. By the time he launched the counter offensive against the Germans at the famous battle of El Alamein in November 1942, he had the benefit of leading the attack with the best tank in the world, the American Sherman. By May 1943, the British army had reversed their earlier territorial losses and effectively kicked the Germans out of North Africa.

Whilst a great General and great tactics would have made a big difference, it is possible that one of the deciding factors in the battles had to be the better tanks, a direct result of Churchill's desire for a detailed understanding of tank warfare. Apart from a few hiccups, the Allied habit of winning continued until they rode into Berlin in 1945.

In trying to use examples from my own experiences to attempt to put the chapters into a modern context, it is difficult to come up with anything that does not pale into insignificance in comparison with Churchill. If I am being brutally honest with myself, I am not the world's best example of someone who keeps to the habit of managing the detail enough. At the same time, it is impossible to manage all the detail of a business all the time without everything coming to a grinding halt.

In reality, it is best to manage as much of the detail as possible, taking a balanced view, making compromises on occasions whilst sticking to the important things.

I mentioned in an earlier chapter how I had been asked in a previous company to set up a new business based on my industry experience. I had a very clear idea of what I wanted and what requirements customers had. One of the crucial elements was to ensure that the service was web based and fully automated. I did not want humans involved in the processes whatsoever, being a great believer that the less people in a process, the greater the reliability of the service.

It would have been very easy in the early stages to rush it out to market and capture some business as a result of compromises on delivery and the details behind the service. If I had stuck 100% to every single detail, the service would have taken eighteen months to launch and not the six months required to meet the business plan. I had meeting after meeting and battle after battle making sure my vision of the service and its core operation remained consistent. In reality I had to compromise on occasions, apart from anything else, no one would have wanted to work with me if I didn't. I can remember on a number of occasions having really heated discussion with different people in the business, because I wanted to stick to what I thought was right.

I lost count of the number of times something was not possible, only to find a solution myself and then take it back to the person who said no, for implementation.

Churchill used to infuriate the different wartime departments because he would not necessarily believe what they told him. He relied on his own knowledge and a number of people he really trusted to double check things if he was not confident in what people were telling him.

After the service was launched to customers a number of bugs were discovered. I was the developers' worst nightmare as I refused to allow issues to drag on in the way they usually did. I insisted that the issue took priority and was fixed in a timely manner.

By holding on to what I wanted and not compromising on the important details, I managed to launch a service which was market leading and which went on to be incredibly successful, delivering in excess of £100M worth of business.

On another occasion I once worked under a senior manager who was without doubt the closest I have come to working with someone who had a "Churchillian" attention to detail. He was in charge of a large sales operation responsible for delivering £400M/$800M worth of business. The chap before him was a typical old-fashioned senior manager, delegating in such a way that he did not know much about things happening below him, relying on information from his first line reports. Once a month he would meet with his team for a business update.

Unfortunately, the MD of the company had no confidence in the monthly sales estimates from the previous manager; they derived from best guesses and speculation, and were constantly inaccurate.

The business needed confidence in the estimates from the sales force to enable the rest of the business to correctly scale to meet predicted demand. Too high a forecast and they would waste money, too low and they would be incapable of delivering customer orders on time.

The new senior manager came in and completely shook things up. Out went guesswork and in came new processes and systems, which quickly transformed the accuracy of the forecasts. In addition to the new processes, his approach to business was very similar to Churchill; he was an absolute stickler for detail. Nothing was too small or insignificant for him.

He rigidly enforced adherence to the new processes. This was perceived by the managers who worked for him as a lack of trust, and in reality, despite pleasant words to the contrary, it was probably the case. These after all were the same managers that contributed to the previous regime. In effect, they needed to re earn the trust of the new man. The difference was that the new man wanted to know about everything and appeared to have the capacity to digest and comment on every detail.

Instead of a monthly catch up meeting, every week the first reports would have a two/three hour conference call covering every aspect of the business. This consisted of a report that categorized issues into Red for very serious and business affecting. Yellow for serious issues that needed dealing with and Black for good news big orders etc. The report also had an action list, which covered tasks that needed completing by a certain time. The final element was a detailed list of all the business opportunities over a certain size and a track of business by department, against monthly and yearly targets.

Each manager who was required to attend the call had to do similar calls with the managers who reported to them, to enable them to gather sufficient information to complete the 2/3 hour call. The monthly meeting still took place, going into even more detail, covering planning and development.

A classic example of how he managed business compared to the previous person was when issues were escalated to him. If you had a problem and wanted it raised on the weekly 2/3 hour call for him to help resolve, you would have to provide extensive detail and evidence to prove that you had done everything possible to try to fix it yourself. No escalation was possible unless a thorough investigation had taken place. This approach halted managers pushing issues onto him that should have been resolved had they tried hard enough.

The output of all this change and the approach of managing by detail was a complete turnaround in the fortunes of the company. Confidence was restored in the sales organization enabling the planners to accurately build capacity and recruit staff.

After a great deal of initial hostility it had the same effect on the company as Churchill had when he took over as Prime Minister. Everyone knew they couldn't get away with being sloppy anymore and this completely changed the culture of the business for the better.

The senior manager was one of those rare people who combined good business talents with an affable nature and a ruthless streak. He had the desire and capacity to work fourteen hours a day, enabling him to deliver relentless management of the detail. Not everyone has this level of desire matched in equal measure by capability, everyone is different and what works for one person will not be suitable for someone else.

He was the first senior manager I worked under who took this approach to business. When he joined the business, I had a similar reaction to the other managers who were used to larger-than-life sales directors who oozed charisma. Whilst the new systems and procedures were difficult to get used to, at no point did I feel that he was introducing anything that prevented the sales teams from performing. The methods were just so completely different to anything I had seen before. It is only now some years later, whilst reflecting on my past for the purposes of this chapter that I realize how good he was, and the similarity of his approach to business with that of Churchill's methods for managing the detail of war.

Managing the detail for most people is sort of a habit and like good and bad habits, there is a tendency to drift in and out of them. Even Churchill, who at the outset of the war was probably the greatest practitioner of managing detail in the world, had his moments later on in the war when he wasn't quite as effective as in those early days. No one is perfect and it is unlikely that many can manage all of the detail all of the time, like the senior manager. What comes across loud and clear from Churchill is the more you practice managing detail the more good flows from it.

Chapter 6

Negotiate Hard for Your Convictions

By the time I had finished reading Churchill's memoirs, my original admiration for America had considerably increased. I had heard of Roosevelt but it was only through Churchill that I discovered what a truly great man he was. Especially the way he stood by Churchill and Britain throughout the dark early days of the war. Europe and Britain owe him the most immense debt of gratitude.

There was a time, between June 1940 after the fall of France and December 1941 before Pearl Harbor, when Britain stood alone as the last surviving democracy in Europe, determined to stand up to the mighty Germans who had the Italians and Russians backing them. All desperate to see the downfall of Britain and its Empire and resolved to carve up pieces for themselves. Churchill knew Britain needed to survive until the Americans somehow joined the war as Germany could not have been defeated without their help.

By November 1940, Britain was broke; having used up the bulk of foreign reserves buying weapons of war, principally from the USA. Britain had sold off any companies operating in America for the best price they could get. Courtaulds was a well-known example. Britain was burning through money at an unsustainable rate; you cannot win a war if you do not have the weapons and this requires money in plentiful supply.

Roosevelt struggled to persuade the American people about the benefit of spending $billions helping Britain.

In June 1940, the USA was so certain that Britain would lose to Germany that they asked for all the British Navy ships and munitions be sent across the Atlantic to stop them being used against America after the Nazi's inevitably crushed Britain. Churchill told Roosevelt to take a hike.

Churchill wrote to Roosevelt alerting him of the impending crisis. He pointed out that if Britain could not be sustained due to lack of arms and in particular, a lack of the imported essentials needed to feed the people, then America would be next. Churchill's negotiation position at this point might on the face of it, have seemed very weak, however, by proving to Roosevelt that without Britain's survival America would suffer a terrible fate; the problem became a shared one, which they both needed to resolve.

It was not realistic for the Americans to lend money to Britain; the amount would be so large that repayment would be impossible. The American constitution prevented Roosevelt from just giving Britain the desperately needed arms. Roosevelt and his aides delved into history and discovered the lend lease bill, passed in 1894. Lend Lease was at once brilliant and easy for Roosevelt to explain to the American public. In Roosevelt's, own words, "imagine your neighbor's house catches fire and your neighbor needs to borrow your hose to put it out. You don't wait until your neighbor gives you the fifteen dollars, the hose cost, before giving it to him, you lend it on the basis that he will give you the hose back when he has put out the fire." This in simplicity is what Roosevelt did for Britain, he loaned Britain all the planes, tanks, ships and guns that America could make, using its vast production capacity. Britain did not have to pay for any of this vital equipment; it was on loan until the end of the war. What remained in working order would be returned by a grateful nation.

At a single stroke, Britain's prospects improved dramatically. This act of generosity borne out of principled self-interest should be remembered forever, both in Britain and throughout Europe. To get America to this point took a tremendous effort of negotiation and persuasion from Churchill. Sadly the British minister who conducted the talks in Washington on his behalf, died shortly after the policy became public.

Without Lend Lease, Britain would almost certainly have perished. Churchill persuaded Roosevelt that if Britain lost the war against Germany, then it would only be a matter of time until the USA suffered at the hands of the Germans, both in terms of trade and militarily. The Germans would then have possessed the largest Navy in the world and the whole war making capacity of Europe and Russia. Even without Japan, they could have potentially held the USA to ransom, strangling international trade, leading to economic collapse in the USA.

After the Germans had consolidated their position in Europe, they could have attacked Canada and Mexico landing vast armies with little opposition over a period of time. They could have then attacked the USA from multiple positions along the Canadian border, whilst simultaneously attacking southern America via Mexico aiming for the Texas oil fields. This offensive could have been coordinated with a Japanese attack on Hawaii. Giving the Japanese the opportunity to capture the Island and use it as a base for further attacks against the west coast of America. However it happened, WWII would have eventually landed up on America's door step.

Roosevelt understood that Lend Lease wasn't just about helping Britain; it was to protect America's short and long-term security interests. Britain fought to save herself whilst simultaneously protecting America from ruin.

At the beginning of the War, British scientists had been working on the development of a new type of bomb, the Atom bomb. The team went under the code name of "The Department for Tube Alloys". British scientists where convinced that they could build a bomb in time to have an effect on the war. Shortly after Pearl Harbor Churchill had the first combined war conference in Washington, he took with him the key nuclear scientists.

Coincidentally American scientists had been working on the theory of building an Atom bomb, however, in Churchill's view they lagged behind the British. Churchill was resolved to build a bomb. He did not want it built in Britain as German bombing or agents could have destroyed it at any time. He designated Canada as the place for developing the bomb; it was far safer with the potential for greater secrecy.

The estimated cost of building the bomb in 1941 was £500M, the equivalent of £10BN in today's money. No small sum, for cash strapped Britain. Churchill managed to persuade America to pay for the development. He scheduled a meeting with Roosevelt and the British scientists; they convinced the president that it was possible to build a bomb in time to have an influence on the war. Churchill then negotiated an agreement, enabling British scientists to pool their research and work on the bomb, subject to the sharing of future developments and knowledge. This was no small achievement; he not only persuaded the US to develop a bomb, but also made sure that Britain kept up with the development of future nuclear weapons. The Manhattan Project was born.

Without Churchill's negotiating skills there would not have been a Hiroshima or Nagasaki. Based on Churchill's memoirs he believed that without dropping at least one of the two bombs on Japan the Japanese would not have surrendered. This would have probably led to the deaths of hundreds of thousands more Allied and Japanese soldiers. According to Churchill, the Emperor was determined to see every soldier dead rather than surrender. The allies could well have believed this at the time, as the Japanese had been the early practitioners of suicide bombing, by way of Hari Kiri, the practice of flying planes into Allied warships; in addition, the army regularly committed ritual suicide rather than surrender.

After the Allied victory over Germany, Churchill was gravely concerned that the Russians were going to occupy most of Europe. The Russians had gone from allies of the Germans at the beginning of the war to impoverished underdogs at the point in June 1941 when the Germans turned against them and opened up an eastern front. Everyone assumed the might of the German army would quickly crush the Russians. However, they became conquering heroes who considerably reduced the length of the war by destroying large parts of the German army on the eastern front. Churchill was convinced that the Soviets wanted to set up pseudo Russian governments in all the countries they occupied, effectively making them Russian satellites. They had already managed this in Poland with the Lublin government, contradicting the agreement they had made at both the Tehran and Yalta conferences. History proved Churchill correct.

At the Potsdam conference after victory in Europe, the Russians attempted to take more of Europe than was originally agreed between the allies. They expected to strong arm the USA into concessions as they were convinced that America needed Russian help to defeat Japan. Shortly into the conference, news came through to Churchill and Truman (who had taken over from Roosevelt) that the "babies had been born".(the two bombs that dropped on Japan were subsequently code named Little Boy and Big Boy). This was the code for announcing the successful testing of an atom bomb in the Arizona dessert. This simple message heralded the birth of the nuclear age.

Shortly afterwards Churchill had a private meeting with Stalin and explained the development. The Russians would have quickly understood the ramifications of the western allies owning the first weapon of mass destruction.

Whatever the long-term view of the bombs development, it made the negotiating stance of the western allies far easier than it would have been. The Americans did not have to rely on Russian help to defeat Japan and therefore did not need to make unnecessary concessions.

Given the amount of research taking place in both Britain and America, the development of a bomb was a certainty. Because of Churchill's hard negotiating stance in January 1942, the bomb was able to have a material effect on the outcome of the war in Japan, and on peace in Europe.

Another example of Churchill negotiating hard for what he believed in, was stopping Greece going the way of Poland and becoming a communist state. Unlike the Atom Bomb negotiations, which were carried out in secret, this cost over a thousand British lives and initially proved very unpopular in both Britain and America. Churchill received a lot of bad press at the time for what people assumed to be one monarchy supporting another. Greece held a special significance for him as Britain had made great sacrifices in 1941, sending 50,000 troops to help them defend their soil from the Germans & Italians. The operation failed, resulting in the deaths of thousands of Allied troops.

Churchill had become exasperated with the Greek resistance, made up of two factions; one was loyal to the king and democracy, the other was communist, assisted by the Soviets. Britain offered help to both groups, the common enemy was German and anyone who would fight the Germans deserved support. Unfortunately, the two factions seemed more intent on fighting each other than fighting the enemy.

Churchill had negotiated a deal with Stalin that in return for Britain keeping out of Polish affairs the Soviets would keep out of Greece. Britain's settlement with Stalin assumed Poland would be a free democratic state and not the Soviet puppet regime it became.

By October 1944, Churchill had become aware of the style of democracy Stalin promoted when the Red Army occupied a country. He was deeply concerned that Greece would end up as another Soviet backed government. Churchill took steps to keep a large British force near to Greece ready to move in once the Germans had evacuated.

In November 1944 he ordered five thousand British troops to take control of Athens. The British had to fight street by street to wrestle control of the Greek capital from the communists. According to Churchill, Stalin had not double-crossed him by actively backing the communists, it was the faction themselves that were bent on taking over the country. However, had they succeeded, the Soviets would have soon had their hands on the levers of Greek power.

After taking control of Athens and the surrounding area, the British commanders on the ground told Churchill it would be impossible to clear Greece of communists without committing vast amounts of additional troops, which simply was not practical. He was convinced that the only solution was a negotiated settlement. The Greek factions detested each other and in Churchill's view if you left a Greek man alone in a room, he would pick an argument with himself.

It was Christmas Eve December 1944, the last Christmas of the War. Clementine, Churchill's wife had everything arranged and all the family and an array of guests were at Chequers, the country retreat for British Prime Ministers. The beautifully decorated tree, cut down from Roosevelt's own special forest at his private house, was shipped over as it had been since 1941. It is difficult to imagine how angry Clementine must have been when Churchill walked in and said, "I am not going to be home for Christmas I am off to Greece to save it from Communism".

Clementine would have recognized the worthy nature of the mission but I doubt many wives would be very understanding in such circumstances. Off Churchill flew to Greece with a small entourage.

Churchill's memoirs contain a significant amount of text detailing the Greek situation. By going to Greece, he demonstrated to the protagonists, that he was deadly serious about resolving the issue. He put all the factions together in a room on Christmas day; he literally would not let them leave the room until they had thrashed out an agreement. Armed guards blocked the exit.

Churchill had identified the impressive figure of Archbishop Damaskinos as a good man to act as leader, although he had initially been a bit skeptical about him.

After long hours of heated discussion, agreement was reached. A few days later the London based King of Greece appointed Damaskinos head of the government. Greece (courtesy of direct intervention from Churchill) did not end up going the way of

Poland, Romania, Czechoslovakia and Hungary.

Churchill firmly believed that there was no point winning the war if you could not offer a lasting democratic peace. He knew by December 1944 that Britain could not save Poland from communism. Greece however was different, as Britain had greater forces available to help determine a successful outcome.

Before reading Churchill's memoirs, I had no idea that he had saved Greece from communism or that over 1000 British service men had died in the process. Churchill's commitment to what he believed in and his tough stance with the Greeks, despite the bad press he received, ultimately saved Greece from the miserable fate of Poland. Thankfully, this situation finally resolved itself satisfactorily after many years.

A small example of my own persistence was when at one of the companies I worked for I launched an incentive program to take a group of customers on a business incentive to Dubai. It was entirely my idea and if the incentive failed, totally my responsibility. I was confident that the customers we dealt with would seize the opportunity to win an all expenses paid trip to Dubai, the day had long passed when such incentives were commonplace in my industry. The plan with the incentive was to direct new business to my company instead of the competition. This worked assuming our service and pricing was in line with other industry offerings.

It launched in October, the winners needed to qualify by the following March. The incentive was a resounding failure, instead of twenty winners bringing in lots of business, five winners delivered about one third of anticipated sales. Thankfully, only a small amount of money required spending before the number of winners became apparent. Such a disappointment would normally led to an embarrassing moment of explanation and a hasty plan to minimize the fall out. We could have sent the few winners to Dubai or given them some money and cancelled it. Instead, I decided to push for the incentive to be re-launched. The feedback I had received during the incentive was almost entirely positive.

Whilst the customers were keen in principle, they were also lethargic. I assumed the trip was so good it would sell itself, which it clearly had not. I was certain that with a greater degree of promotion from the sales teams, it would work.

After countless meetings, conference calls and E-mails I managed to convince the company to carry the original budget for the incentive over to the following year and give me another chance. The trip was re-designed, the qualification criteria was changed delivering improved engagement for customers and more profit for the business. I ensured the sales team focused more on the incentive and constantly hounded everyone to promote the trip effectively.

The second time the incentive was a resounding success, delivering millions in extra business for the company. Dubai is a great location for a short company incentive and all twenty customers had a brilliant time. The success of the second attempt, made all the hard work of persuading the company to give me a second chance worthwhile.

One of the surprising aspects of the trip was how well relationships developed with customers. The incentive trip was to be purely for pleasure, with an unwritten rule that no "work" discussion was to take place, in such a relaxed atmosphere it was easy to form business friendships.

Customers expect suppliers to cynically use such events to form relationships for their own benefit, which was genuinely not the plan with the trip. The customers were great; everyone had a fantastic time, making it very easy for me as a host to get to know everyone. It is easy to show civility to anyone, but it is difficult to fake genuine friendliness over a period of five days when you are constantly in each other's company.

After the trip, I have lost count of the number of times that these close relationships proved beneficial for both the customers and myself. Something I would never have predicted, a very definite, but tangible benefit of the incentive.

It is embarrassing, trying to describe a scenario from my ordinary life, to highlight an example of a Churchill technique. In one sense, the examples are insignificant compared to negotiations for an atomic bomb or saving a country from communism. In another, the same principal applies, whether it is for a bomb or a business incentive. If you really believe in something, you should negotiate and persuade as hard as possible to achieve it.

Chapter 7

Your Own Words Can Make a Tasty Dish

As you get older you discover it is not a disaster to change a course of action, if it results from a wrong decision or fresh information, leading to a re-evaluation of a business strategy.

At sixty-five when he took control of the war, Churchill knew this very well. Clearly, no one makes decisions or plans believing they are wrong. Unfortunately too many people, once they have decided on a plan, see it as a weakness or the cause of lost pride or integrity to change their mind.

Churchill would not advocate somebody constantly chopping and changing, trying to do business with such people would be incredibly difficult, however there will be times and they will hopefully be rare, that for any number of reasons, plans have to be abandoned or a strategy radically altered.

Churchill took the view that abandoning a broken plan at the earliest opportunity was the better for everyone concerned. Carrying on when there is an obvious problem and hoping for the best is a recipe for disaster. Far better to acknowledge a mistake, make any necessary explanation, apologize and take the medicine. Trying to brave it out in the face of probable failure or the hope of a change in circumstances is neither a plan nor a strategy.

Shortly before France surrendered to the Germans, Britain desperately tried to keep them fighting, apart from anything else, the British still had 400,000 troops and associated equipment in France. Without the return of the troops, defending Britain against the inevitable German assault would have been very difficult.

A plan to incorporate France into the union of Great Britain emerged, effectively creating a country under one government, based in London, which included France and all the French dominions.

A 300-word charter was drawn up offering French people the opportunity to become citizens of Great Britain. It was hoped that if they became British whilst Britain was still unconquered, they might be more determined to fight on. The French army would join the British and, more importantly, the French Navy would come under British control. The charter, proposed to the French Prime Minister at a meeting outside Paris, received brief consideration but was quickly re-buffed. The plan was rejected for plenty of reasons, a couple of which were the likelihood Hitler would be harder on the French for agreeing to such a proposal, plus their suspicion that Britain might be looking to expand the Empire by taking control of French colonies as a result of the deal.

It now seems completely implausible that the French would accept such an offer, but in those dark days of early 1940, desperate men took desperate measures.

After the French prime minister refused the offer, rather than press ahead with the plan, Churchill dropped it, even though a great deal of effort had gone into preparing the charter for the French people. It was far better to recognize the plan as a dud and move on than to try to persuade the French people directly once their Prime Minister had effectively given up control to the Germans.

Towards the end of the war, there were competing interests for how best to take the fight to the Germans. One plan was to invade Norway, almost by way of revenge for the British getting a German thrashing there in the early days of 1940. Britain had tried to invade Norway to prevent the Germans getting access to Norwegian iron ore.

The big issue was how to position sufficient air power off the coast of Norway to assist in the landings. Given how thinly spread the navy was, the allies could not have amassed enough aircraft carriers to give a landing sufficient chance of success. Without airpower it would have been a non-starter.

A British inventor had come up with a process that mixed ice with wood chippings, which when frozen created an incredibly tough material that took a long time to defrost. Churchill liked the idea so much, that he decided to demonstrate it to the Joint Chiefs of Staff.

Everyone was sitting in the secret meeting, the inventor brought in a block of ice that had been subject to the new process. To demonstrate its strength Churchill pulled out a pistol and fired a shot at the block of ice. The material was so strong that it ricocheted off the ice and just missed one of the US Generals. At which point the security guards came rushing in thinking there had been an assassination attempt. Thankfully, all was well.

Everyone was impressed with the invention. The plan, which looking back could be considered ambitious to say the least (but I suppose you could use the phrase "he who dares, wins" about it), was to break off a chunk of glacier from the Arctic. After flattening it and applying the wood pulp process, tugboats would then tow it to the Norwegian coast. It would transform into a giant floating airfield, capable of accommodating enough planes to enable an attack to take place.

You have to consider when judging the plan that this was the same country which conceived, and built, the bouncing bomb, which destroyed a significant part of the Ruhr valley industrial production, though no one thought that the huge structure of a dam could be bombed successfully.

Churchill pressed ahead with the development of the floating airfield project and a large team was put together to examine the practicalities of putting the plan into action. At the point when it became clear the allies would not be invading Norway, Churchill quickly took the decision to bury it. There was no point wasting valuable time and resources on something, even though it had the attraction of being so unique that to pull it off would have been a tremendous achievement.

It would have been a remarkable sight, an enormous great flattened iceberg with an airfield cut into the middle. Imagine the photographs and archive footage. You could just see the faces of the Germans defending the Norwegian coast as this great big flat white object floated into place bristling with hundreds of spitfires and bombers.

Churchill was tremendously keen on seeing the idea come to fruition but once the circumstances changed, he had the courage to drop it.

Some years ago, I worked as a marketing manager for a company manufacturing and selling laser printers, among other things. I was responsible for the creation of marketing plans to promote the printers in the UK and across Europe.

For a long time we had been desperate for a low cost, high speed, black and white laser printer. The company specialized in big printers, but by offering a low-end printer at the right price we could open the door to more customers and then introduce the higher end machines to them.

Finally, product development created a printer that fitted the requirement. We put together a huge plan to market the printer across Europe with a very big six-figure budget. We set the PR team to work, ten different countries had new adverts created and space was booked in magazines all across Europe.

This was all taking place in November; everyone was excited, finally we could take the business to the next level. The campaign was high profile with the CEO of Europe taking an active interest. Thousands upon thousands of the printers were stacked high in the newly automated warehouse. We received the go-ahead; adverts were booked for the January editions of relevant magazines. The competition did not have a clue what was going to hit them. They would be ashen faced and left floundering once the campaign hit the streets. It was over for them they just did not know it yet. At least that is what we thought!

About mid November I started to get a few disturbing reports about how well the printers were performing. I set up a team to find out what was going on. After exhaustive testing, we discovered the most bizarre thing I had yet encountered in my business career. If a customer switched off the printer at night and the office it was in got cold, the first 10 pages the printer churned out in the morning were completely solid black. This did not happen if the printer stayed switched on, or if the office heating stayed on overnight, clearly a problem.

Because the printer's target market was small business, the sort that would probably switch the printer and the heating off to save on energy bills, we realized by early December that we had a big issue. There was no way we could fix the printers in time for the campaign. A crunch decision was required, press on knowing we would be selling faulty printers, or take the brave decision to pull the campaign. We could then fix the printers and try again in three of four months.

If I had stayed true to Churchill's principle of the chapter, I would have bravely insisted that we pull the campaign and taken it on the chin, whilst blaming the manufacturer of the printer for the issues. All would have been well and I could have re-launched the campaign in the early spring confident in the re-engineered printer. With hindsight, which is one of the very few exact sciences, this is what should have happened, but it did not.

I put the issue to my boss who then raised it with the head of marketing for Europe I also made sure I had an e-mail chain to cover myself if everything went wrong, which it did, in a big way. (Incidentally, when Churchill was a soldier and was commanded to pass military orders to other officers he always insisted on having them in writing). The decision was made at a very high level to press on with the campaign, sell thousands of printers and hope that not too many ended up in cold offices. As mentioned earlier, hope is neither a plan nor a strategy and in this particular case, luck was not on our side.

By February we were inundated with printers that we knew had a problem before we sold them. A plan was put in place to get them swapped by the manufacturer for new ones. The strategy was to brave it out until April when we relied on the weather warming up to stop the flow of returns, which it actually did.

Over the summer, more inventory of cold resistant printers arrived. I am not in a position to give you either a happy ending or any ending for that matter; I decided to leave the company in the August of that year. The debacle of the cold weather printers was the last straw for me.

The problem caused every company that supplied printers on our behalf and every end user that bought one of the printers, to associate my company with the manufacture of rubbish. This did terrible damage to the reputation of the company in that particular market. Support for the good products, that were rare, suffered badly because staff could not cope with the issue of dealing with the cold weather printers.

Sales teams were de-motivated; they spent all their time receiving abuse from their customers for selling them such a bad product. Distributors who had bought the printers to sell on to smaller companies were swamped with complaints and stopped buying any products until the problem was resolved. Finance spent all their time raising credits and could not get cash in from customers, because they refused to pay invoices until credits were raised.

This was overall, an unmitigated disaster and entirely the companies fault. They had the information in time to stop the problem from happening; they could have kept their reputation intact and saved themselves and their employees from a torrid year. Instead, they employed that age-old business strategy of hoping that by some miracle, the problem would just go away and all would be well in the end.

Hindsight is a great thing to have. Years later when writing this chapter it is blindingly obvious that it would all end in disaster unless they had had the equivalent of winning the business lottery. I was much younger and I would like to have been able to write that I heroically stopped the problem before it happened, like some hero from WWII saving the day. In reality I take my share of the blame for letting it happen, I was young, ambitious and keen to progress, rocking the boat too much could have jeopardized my career. Given the same circumstances 10 years on, I would not have let the campaign go ahead and would have gone as high as I needed to get it stopped.

In fairness, it probably did me a favor. It was the last straw for me, and I moved on to another position and started a new career completely out of the printer business. I doubled my income over night, much to the satisfaction of my wife. I also saw a lot more of my children growing up.

Churchill would have pulled the campaign without hesitation.

Chapter 8

Avoid Being a Slave to Technology

Churchill was passionate about inventions and the development of new technology that could help win the war. His experience had also taught him that whilst new technology could be a powerful aid it was not a solution in itself.

There are some great examples of the influence a new technology had on the outcome of the war. However, the deciding factor for Churchill was the practical deployment against the enemy, and the realistic measurement of its success. He placed more importance on these aspects than on the invention itself.

Historians would class the Battle of Britain technically, as a score draw. The French had surrendered; the Germans were using Northern France for what was to be the second to last stop, on the way to complete domination of Europe.

Hitler had very successfully employed a program of one victory at a time. He would firstly promise his target country that he would not invade them, then did exactly that, whilst promising the neighboring country that he would not invade them, and so on. This carried on until Western Europe had been conquered leaving just Russia and Great Britain to be sorted out. The German codename for the invasion of Great Britain was operation Sea Lion, whilst the Russians would eventually lose millions of lives, but ultimately defend themselves, against operation Barbarossa.

One of the big differences between the First and Second World

War was the importance of air power in battle. The British had learned a harsh lesson when in February 1940 they had tried to force a landing in Norway. The plan had been to prevent the Germans from getting access to Norway's vast supplies of iron ore. This was a strategic target, whichever country could produce the greater quantity of steel would be the most likely to win the War. The British tried to make a landing against well-fortified German positions without protection from the air; Norway was beyond the reach of fighter cover at the time. Many Royal Navy ships were sunk, the whole operation was a disaster and effectively caused Chamberlain to hand over the leadership to Churchill.

The British soon learned that a land battle or a sea engagement near to shore would be difficult to win, without a minimum of parity in the air. Successfully forcing a landing against well-fortified positions would require air superiority.

For Germany to conquer Britain they needed to dominate the English sky, the Luftwaffe's attempt to gain air supremacy was the beginning of the Battle of Britain. Without victory in the air, they would not have been able to mount an invasion using a vast armada of boats laden with hundreds of thousands of troops and tanks as it would have exposed them to tremendous risk. In the summer of 1940 German soldiers were accustomed to success, they were yet to taste defeat and were by far the best-prepared and armed fighting machine in the world at the time. Had they succeeded it was a distinct possibility that England would have gone the same way as France, despite the rhetoric of "fighting to the last man standing".

Hitler probably joked with his generals on hearing threatened countries say they would fight to the death, just before they surrendered. The reality in my own uneducated opinion is that Britain, when faced with overwhelming odds, and the successful landing on British soil of such a huge and deadly force, would have eventually capitulated.

Had Operation Sea lion achieved its objective, the Germans would have had access to all of Britain's military production, converting the factories for their own use, just like the rest of conquered Europe. The Germans would have taken over the British Navy, the second largest navy in the world at the time. They would have then launched operation Barbarossa and conquered Russia. America could not have supplied the vital aid to Russia, which helped them defeat the Nazi's, without a free Britain. At which point Hitler would have had control of a large part of the planet. Over time, in alliance with Japan, they could have picked off every other country except America. Potentially leaving the USA to financial collapse and forcing some sort of negotiated agreement, a dreadful outlook for the world in June 1940.

This nightmare did not become a reality, because of the effective use of available technology and home advantage. Britain, inspired by Lord Beaverbrook, the minister in charge of aircraft production, had managed by a massive effort to build up a large quantity of Spitfires in anticipation of the air battle. Beaverbrook was able to keep production going during the conflict at sufficient levels to replace a large proportion of the damaged fighters.

The German Messerschmitt was technically faster than the Spitfire, had excellent, accurate guns and therefore should have been able to beat the world's most famous plane. The Meshersmitt had a problem; it was only faster than the Spitfire at high altitude and could not stay in a dogfight for more than about ten minutes without needing to return to France to re-fuel. The British engineers had specifically designed the Spitfire for dog fighting and optimized them for low altitude. The British strategy was to make the Germans stay low where they had the advantage.

The home team had other benefits, pilots could stay longer in the air and if shot down, they were more likely to survive and fly again. German pilots bailing out would spend the rest of their time in a British POW camp. One of the door attendants at a club Churchill frequented, remarked using a football analogy, "I see we've made it to another European Championship final and it's to be played on home ground" The British have a great tradition of cracking jokes when in the most mortal danger!

Britain used radar technology for the first time in the war. Churchill had made great efforts to get a whole series of radar stations put in place before the battle began. This gave the RAF the ability to predict where the Germans would attack and enabled the scrambling of fighters to intercept the enemy.

This combination of fighter design and radar, combined with the skill and courage of the fighter pilots, made the German task a difficult one. The battle raged in the skies between August and October and was a desperately close fought business. At one key point in the middle of September, at the very peak of the fighting, Churchill made a visit to air command. He was talking to the head of the RAF and was being shown by map, the deployment of fighters in the air. Churchill asked what reserves were on the ground and where they were stationed. The Air Marshall told him that every serviceable fighter was currently in the air and there were no more reserves. Given that all the fighters were engaged in dogfights with the Germans, it would be fair to call it a pivotal day in world history.

Historians would say that despite claims at the time that the British shot down three German planes for the loss of each one of theirs, in reality, the ratio was closer to one for one. Britain was able to produce more planes per month than the Germans and eventually the Germans had to stop, otherwise they would have had insufficient fighters to defend the homeland from bomber attack by the British.

At the battles of Trafalgar, Waterloo and Blenheim after long preparation the issue settled itself in a few days; the Battle of Britain however, lasted about two months from start to finish. It started slowly in August, reached a peak in September and petered out in October.

Churchill detailed in his book how the Germans made a strategic error during the Battle of Britain, letting Britain off the hook when they were most vulnerable. Towards the end of August, the Germans had become increasingly effective at bombing the runways of the southern fighter airbases. So much so, that it was becoming almost impossible to station sufficient fighters to deal with the ever-increasing threat from the air.

It reached a critical point, the RAF had about one day left when they had enough serviceable airfields to effectively station fighters to defend Britain from the Luftwaffe, then all of a sudden the bombing of the airbases stopped and the Germans started heavily bombing London instead.

Churchill is convinced that had the Germans continued bombing the airbases, instead of diverting to London, they could well have won the Battle of Britain

Churchill coined the very apt phrase that "never has so much been owed by so many to so few". He got it absolutely spot on, when you consider that something like one thousand British and Allied pilots were responsible for forcing a draw in a battle where a draw was a good result. Those one thousand pilots, using their courage and skill, along with the best that British technology had to offer at the time, saved the western world from an unimaginably grim future.

Hitler liked his technology and boasted that Germany was developing some seriously advanced weaponry, which he believed would help them win the war. This reliance on technology was to prove part of his undoing in the end.

The Germans put huge resources into developing the V1 flying bomb and the V2 rocket. They did this because they calculated that the British would not have an effective response to a fast flying bomb, which they eventually did, and to the V2 rocket, which Hitler correctly predicted could not be stopped. It came straight out of the sky plummeting vertically at over a thousand miles an hour.

The V1 and V2 were the most advanced military technology of their time; the problem was each V1 cost eight times more than a fighter plane to produce and took twice as long. Similarly the V2 rockets cost 20 times more and took 6 times longer to construct. If Hitler had not been obsessed with developing the rockets and concentrated on the most effective use of resources to support the war effort, he would have been better off making fighters and bombers. Instead, the dazzle of using the latest technology to develop new and sophisticated weapons turned his head. The planes however would have enabled the Germans to improve the defense of France from attack by the allies, making the Allied task of achieving air superiority before Normandy, much harder.

When the V1 bombs started dropping in London they initially caused great panic. They were indiscriminate and very inaccurate, the random nature of the bombing caused great concern to Londoners. At least with the V1 the pulsing noise from the jet engine meant that you could hear it coming, which is where the name of doodlebug came from. The V2 rocket on the other hand was so quick it made no sound.

Initially London's air defenses struggled to cope. It was difficult for a fighter to shoot a V1 down mid-air and anti aircraft guns could not hit them because they were small and fast. Luckily at about the same time, the British were supplied by the USA with a new anti-aircraft proximity shell, which used a magnetic fuse that would explode when it came close to a V1, reducing the requirement for pinpoint accuracy. The Americans perfected the proximity shell technology from research carried out by British scientists earlier in the war.

In an incredible piece of planning and logistics, over a weekend, the British moved all the anti aircraft guns from the outskirts of London to the coast. This involved laying 10,000 miles of phone cable and electrical wire and was a staggering feat of engineering.

The British were then able to shoot down about 90% of the V1's as they came across the coast from France. The Germans could not understand how Britain had become so accurate all of a sudden. It was easier to shoot down the V1's than a fighter or bomber as they flew in a straight line. With the help of new technology from the USA, Britain was able to master the V1 bombs. This effectively neutralized them as a threat and made all of Hitler's research, time, effort and cost associated with the V1 development, almost pointless. Without it however, the introduction of modern Jet planes would have taken considerably longer.

It was all well and good Hitler using this amazing technology, however, it was far more expensive to produce and actually was not that effective in terms of the damage it could cause. It transpired that ordinary high explosive bombs dropped conventionally from the air at a much lower cost, killed more people and caused more damage. Hitler must have hoped the new weapons would have so terrified the British public, that they would force Churchill to seek peace terms.

It was impossible to mount a defense against the V2, it killed randomly. It was said that if you heard the explosion from a V2 then you were still alive. The war office was concerned about the public reaction to the V2 and tried to keep the cause of the explosions secret, blaming them on burst gas mains. The Germans were upset that their new weapon of terror was staying hidden from the British public so they leaked news of the attacks to the New York Times, which was then picked up by the British press. These silent killers carried about the same payload as a V1 but were the most effective weapon developed during the war, except for the Atom Bomb.

Unfortunately, for Germany it was too little, too late. The cost and the resources required to make V2's effectively stole capability from ordinary aircraft research and production. This took valuable capacity away from the defense of the army on the ground. The technology and its wondrous potential had seduced Hitler. He bet everything on it and it cost him dearly. By not being able to defend the army with greater numbers of combat aircraft, the allies overran Germany before Hitler could build enough rockets to make a real difference to the outcome of the war.

Whilst the technology was far in advance of the allies, as Churchill had learned, technology alone would not win a war.

October 1940, the Battle of Britain had ended and Germany had set their sights on bombing Britain into submission, in particular hitting the weapon production factories around the UK. To do this effectively, the Germans developed a method of targeting their conventional bombers using radio beams directed from different parts of Europe towards the UK. Pointing the radio beams in such a way, that they crossed over the exact location of the targets. By using radio detection technology, the German pilots just had to wait until they got the correct signal and then press a button.

Through their network of spies, the British found out about the radio direction bombing and set about trying to foil it. They did not want to jam the signals as the Germans would then know the British were onto them. By amplifying one of the radio signals the British were able to re-direct the German Bombers who then unknowingly dropped their bombs safely over open countryside. Eventually the Germans realized that their systems had been compromised.

The Germans then came up with another type of radio directional technology called Knickerbein, which was a far more sophisticated method of directing the bombers. This new technology based on radio pulses, was now even more accurate and meant that the German bombers could fly and drop bombs in bad weather, thus preventing British fighters from engaging them or anti aircraft guns from shooting them down. This could have left Britain defenseless to accurate bombing whenever the weather was bad, a pretty regular occurrence in Britain.

A young British scientist suspected the development of the Knickerbein. He pieced together information from many different sources, and found that his suspicions were confirmed when a German bomber pilot was shot down and interrogated about the new radio equipment in his plane. After a few months of research, the Knickerbein technology was mastered by the British. For a while, the German bombers would fly at night in bad weather and drop their bombs, thinking that they were destroying factories. The British would light a huge fire after a raid tricking the German Pilots into thinking that they had successfully hit their targets. One friend of Churchill's commented that on a weekend vacation in the country he had seen a hundred German bombers unload a thousand bombs onto an open field in the middle of nowhere. Churchill just smiled knowingly, but could not explain this phenomenon, as very few people knew what the brilliant British scientists had achieved.

At the same time during the war, Churchill was becoming increasingly annoyed with the Irish. They had declared neutrality at the beginning of the war and had subsequently denied the British Navy any access to their ports. This caused huge problems for Britain and made it far more difficult to defend the Merchant Navy from the threat of U-Boats in the Atlantic. Churchill was seething about this, especially since the British were still providing subsidies to help Irish farmers, which they could ill afford. Churchill talked about stopping the subsidies but he did not state in his books whether Britain actually followed through on the threat.

Coincidentally, a freak occurrence took place at this time. A large number of German bombers "accidentally" dropped their payload of bombs over Dublin. Churchill deliberately mentioned this incident in the same chapter that he talked about mastering the Knickerbein technology in his memoirs. It would not surprise me if he had instructed the British scientists to direct the German bombers to Dublin, ensuring that the Irish lost confidence in the Germans and to punish them for denying the Navy access to their ports. It just seems most unlikely that even in bad weather the German Pilots would have avoided Britain altogether, accidentally dropping their bombs on Dublin.

The "Battle of the Beams" ended in the summer of 1941, once the Germans invaded Russia. By the time the bombing campaign against Britain was renewed in 1944, new guidance methods rendered the beam technology obsolete.

When I first went into the selling business, I worked for a well-known company selling photocopiers. By the time I joined, their best years were behind them, however, their training was second to none which presented a real opportunity for someone like me with no prior sales experience.

The copiers we sold were expensive compared to the competition.

We had weeks of training to help persuade potential customers that the additional benefits of the advanced technology were just what they needed. The copiers had far greater sophistication than anything the competition had developed; it was easy for a new recruit to be convinced of their superiority after six weeks of residential training.

Most customers want a photocopier to be able to photocopy, in a lot of cases they want to put a piece of paper on the glass or in the feeder, press a button and get out something that looks like the paper they put in. My company's copiers did this; they just did it for a lot more money.

The competitors copiers were not as good, but in reality, they were more than adequate for the job. They cost less, because the manufacturers concentrated on building a copier to the specification the market wanted, at a price the end users would be happy to pay.

We were told to concentrate on how robust our copiers were when selling, and to bring to the customer's attention the rather flimsy nature of the competitors machines. Robustness is a fine quality, if you are using the copiers in a military zone; it is not really a huge differentiator under normal office conditions.

Our copiers could do the most amazing things with paper, once it had exited the copier, stapling, folding, making booklets, you name it, our copiers could do it. Unfortunately for the sales force, the number of customers wanting such functionality was few and far between, most customers just wanted to copy, with the more sophisticated possibly wanting to staple. Something my copiers did and so did our competitors.

I have been in the sales business for nearly twenty years and there will be some salespeople reading this thinking that due to my inexperience I was unable to sell the features and benefits of my machines over the competition, using the age-old salespersons excuse of blaming price. In fact, considering it was my first sales position, I was rather successful; I won an incentive trip to

Bermuda after nine months.

Quick story about Bermuda, Churchill stopped there after his first conference with Roosevelt in early 1941. British Spitfires nearly shot him down on his way back home.

He had flown from Washington to Bermuda in a brand new Boeing flying boat to rendezvous with a battleship for the return journey. He was so impressed with the plane and the pilot that he asked if it would fly him all the way back to Britain. The pilot did a few calculations and confirmed it was possible. After a few arguments, the chiefs of staff agreed that it would be safer to fly home, rather than risk the German subs trying to hunt him down, knowing he had been to America due to the press coverage surrounding the trip.

The Boeing took off and had flown for about eighteen hours after which the Scilly Isles should have been visible but due to low cloud they were not spotted. After a few anxious moments, the pilot was advised to fly north immediately. Had they continued, in another five minutes they would have been flying over the German anti aircraft batteries of northern France. Unfortunately, they were now heading to Britain on the same flight path used by the German bombers. They had to maintain radio silence and could not relate their location, for fear of alerting the Germans. A British Radar station detected them and scrambled four Spitfires to shoot them down. Thankfully, the fighters did not find the Boeing and its precious passenger; it could have been the worst example of shooting down by friendly fire in history.

It is easy with hindsight to see where the problem lay for my old employer, hindsight being a wonderful thing. A radical shake up of production processes and a total re-vamp of the business was required to compete with the new low priced products coming in from the Far East. Something that is easier said than done. When I won my incentive trip, the company chartered a private jumbo jet to fly all the winners from England to Bermuda. This represented a small percentage of the UK direct sales force. Six years later the business did not employ any direct sales people and sold via third parties. Thankfully, even though they are a considerably smaller company, they are still in business today.

Coming from a technical background, I understand how the seduction of the latest technology can be very compelling, almost regardless of cost. Unless evaluation of the actual payoff takes place with an accountant-like ruthlessness, devoid of seduction, then large sums of money can be wasted, chasing a non-existent competitive edge. When in reality less money spent refining existing systems could have delivered a better result.

Churchill had the benefit of hindsight after the war; it was easy to see that had Hitler not been so obsessed with rocket technology and built fighters and bombers in their place, the Germans would have had a far greater chance of defending themselves against the allies. Thankfully, for humanity's sake, this was not the case.

Those scientists who developed Germany's rocket technology were captured by the Russians and the Allies. They went on to help start the space race.

Chapter 9

Stay Passionate for Things you Don't Agree With

Churchill did not always get his way, especially towards the end of the war. A couple of events stand out in his memoirs. The campaign to conquer Italy and the Operation to land troops in the South of France to coincide with the D-Day landings.

After victory in North Africa, Churchill persuaded the Americans to carry on and take Sicily. He then wanted to defeat Mussolini and kick the Germans out of Italy before D-Day. The Americans were against the plan. Churchill wanted to get through Italy to Vienna, before the Russians, as he no longer trusted them. The Americans however were happy to wait. The issue at stake was the preparation for D-Day. The military planners wanted all the troops and landing craft earmarked for D-Day back in Britain, long before the landings. They did not want to risk anything before the big event. Churchill wanted to keep the troops fighting Germans for as long as possible, returning them just in time.

Churchill lost the argument, after victory in Sicily. He struggled to get enough landing craft to go on to Italy. After the landings, thousands of troops went back to England, weakening the ability of the army to break out of the foothold they had created. Eventually they succeeded and fought all the way to Monte Cassino, half way up the leg of Italy, where they met with strong resistance. Just when they needed additional troops, more returned to England, delaying victory by months, much to Churchill's disappointment. Churchill stated on many occasions that he would fully support a majority decision once it was finalized, even if he had argued passionately against it. "If we are going to be fools, then we will make sure we play the part of fools to the utmost of our ability"

Quick anecdote about how desperate the Germans were to kill Churchill. Shortly after the Casablanca conference where Churchill had lost the argument for a more comprehensive Italian campaign, a famous British actor from the forties was tragically killed. Lesley Howard was the star of the famous forties movie "Brief Encounter". He had been holidaying in Lisbon, Portugal, in 1943 and had caught a commercial flight back from Lisbon to London. This coincided with Churchill returning from the Casablanca conference. For reasons that Churchill found difficult to understand, a German spy based in Lisbon spotted a man in a heavy coat wearing a hat similar to his and smoking a cigar. He thought it was Churchill, taking a commercial flight back from the conference on his own. As if! He radioed this information to German fighter command who then dispatched a fighter and shot the plane down, killing everyone and depriving Britain and the world of an immensely talented actor.

Churchill could not believe that the Germans had been so callous and naïve as to shoot down innocent passengers without being certain of the facts. The Germans would have been far better off forcing the plane to land and capturing the person they had mistaken for Churchill, leaving the remaining passengers to complete the journey.

Because the Americans would not support Churchill's attempt to defeat the Germans in Italy he was very frustrated. The denial of men and landing craft from his Italian campaign to support the American project to land an army in the South of France (codenamed operation Anvil) to link up with the soldiers from Normandy, caused Churchill great anxiety. No matter how hard Churchill tried to persuade the Americans that it was a waste of time, they were adamant that it should go ahead. Again, once the decision was final, he fully supported it, ensuring that it received full British cooperation. Even though operation Anvil was successful, Churchill still thought he was right, believing it to be of limited military value, especially when weighed against the sacrifices made in Italy that enabled it to happen.

In business, everyone has an opinion. There are always competing interests and agenda's, decision making often involves compromise. Most employees do not have the luxury of making decisions entirely on their own. Occasionally, the consensus view or an instruction from senior management seems completely wrong. When this happens, there can be a tendency to do the minimum, half-heartedly, using any opportunity to push an alternative view.

In my role as a manager, individuality and discussion is actively encouraged. I am always open to a suggestion that may improve the business process or enhance a project. Even when I have my heart set on a particular program, if someone else can put forward a coherent reason to drop or significantly amended it, then I will change my position. There is no point clinging on to a plan for the sake of pride, in the face of evidence that it will not work. My biggest challenge is implementing a new company policy that I fundamentally disagree with, knowing that as a manager I have no choice. My responsibility is to explain the policy in the best way possible and bring the team with me. Doing this, whilst retaining credibility, can be challenging. Ultimately, an employer pays you to achieve results within a business framework, decided by the board. I always have the option of leaving if I do not want to do the job.

As a manager, I have always admired the spirit and passion for the job as demonstrated by the sales teams I have worked with. If I cannot explain why something needs doing when one of the team disagrees with me, then I will do my best to clarify the situation. On rare occasions, I might have to demand that a team member complete an action, even when I cannot persuade them of a good reason why. This is the point when you need someone to do something they do not agree with, giving it their full commitment without constantly complaining.

During the war, an event in one part of the world would have a knock on effect, thousands of miles away. Only those with an overarching view of all events could possibly foresee the consequences. Sometimes a person who has to do something they disagree with, cannot possibly understand the reasons behind the decision, because they just do not have all the facts. Sometimes in business, you have to trust that for better or worse those above you know what they are doing and just get on with it.

In my view, it takes a lot of discipline, self-confidence and inner strength to demonstrate motivation for something you disagree with. It is easy to grumble and be half-hearted about a decision. The colleagues and managers I enjoy working with most are those who can get on with the job whilst staying positive. These coincidentally, tend to be the most successful people.

Chapter 10

Demonstrate That People Matter

One of the great surprises within Churchill's memoirs was the incredible people skills he demonstrated amidst the unending pressure of war. He never appeared to lose his ability to make those he encountered from all walks of life, feel special. One example stands out for me, the story of Major General Orde Wingate from Edinburgh. If people live on in print then I dedicate this book to the memory of Orde Wingate. He had gained a reputation in the army as leader of the irregulars in Abyssinia. Some years before the war Italy had occupied Abyssinia, whilst Britain and other countries had colonized other parts of Africa during previous centuries, by the 1930's, the world community judged such aggression as wholly unacceptable behavior.

At the outset of WWII, the British gave arms and military support to the Abyssinian people to help them break free from the Italian fascists, which they did successfully. Wingate was a military liaison between the British and the Abyssinian soldiers, advising them on the best way to oust the Italians.

A quick story about Abyssinia, during a business trip to Las Vegas I picked up a taxi from my hotel and whilst driving along I made conversation with the driver who asked me where I was from. I responded Britain, then repeated the question back to him, to find that he was from Abyssinia. "I bet you don't know where Abyssinia is", he exclaimed. "As a matter of fact I do" I replied, and then recounted how the British helped Abyssinia during the war. The taxi driver was absolutely amazed. By chance I had just finished reading the passage in Volume 2 of Churchill's memoirs about how Britain helped Abyssinia during the war. He told me that most Vegas tourists would not normally know on which continent Abyssinia resides.

After a distinguished military career, Wingate went to the Far East to fight the Japanese. At the time, standard military practice was to progress in battle as far as the means of supply would allow. An army requires feeding, watering, and to be supplied with bullets. It can only progress on any scale if the ability to keep supplies flowing to the troops is available. The means of supply determines how many men can go into battle.

Orde Wingate developed a technique for guerrilla warfare against the Japanese that involved dropping a large group of men behind enemy lines whilst creating a line of supply, via airdrops. At the time, this was a radical approach to Jungle warfare and caused havoc for the Japanese. His style of warfare made a significant contribution towards defeating the Japanese in the Burmese jungle at the latter stages of the war. The technique seems obvious now; however, at the time the airplane in warfare was being completely re-evaluated. Larger planes could fly further, with heavier loads, enabling sufficient regular drops of supplies to be a realistic prospect.

Wingate had been in the jungle for months and was on his way back home for a well-deserved break. Churchill heard that he was landing at an airstrip in the early evening, west of London and decided to invite him to dinner, that very night!

Wingate was taken by car to Downing Street, still in the same smelly clothes he'd travelled in on his three day journey, even when he sat down to dinner. Churchill was greatly impressed by Wingate and thought him an exceptional soldier with a great career ahead of him. Wingate was a Zionist and had been talent spotted as a potential candidate to lead an Israeli army after the war. During desert Churchill asked Wingate to travel with him to a conference arranged in Quebec with Roosevelt. It was 9:00pm; the train was to leave in an hour. He told Wingate that one of his staff would organize fresh clothes for the trip.

Wingate readily agreed to Churchill's request to join him on the trip (how could he refuse?), but mentioned that it was a great shame he would not get to see his wife whilst he was on leave. His wife did not even know that he was on British soil. It was two years since they had last seen each other. He had thought of little else on his three-day journey back home.

All Churchill's conferences were top secret with no one outside a small group of planners knowing where or when they would take place, for obvious security reasons. After Wingate left the room, Churchill made a few enquiries and discovered that Mrs. Wingate lived in Edinburgh. He knew that the journey to Quebec involved a train journey to Scapa Flow in Scotland and then a voyage by war ship to Canada.

At this point Churchill demonstrated one of the traits that made him the great person he was. Without telling Major General Wingate, Churchill instructed his private office to contact the Edinburgh police; they knocked on Mrs. Wingate's door at four in the morning and told her to pack a bag for cold weather. Mrs. Wingate did not have a clue why but followed instructions. She was taken to Edinburgh train station where Churchill's special train made a detour to stop and pick her up. It's hard to imagine the joy and surprise she must have gone through, along with a mixture of emotions when seeing her husband for the first time in years. The cloak and dagger nature of the knock in the early morning and then to learn that she is on Churchill's train heading for a week in Quebec. They stayed at the luxury Hotel Chateau Frontenac where the conference took place. Given that everyone lived on rations in Britain, the luxury of the cruise and sumptuous hotel must have been a fantastic treat. Not to mention the opportunity to spend some "quality time" with her husband in luxurious surroundings.

I can recommend the hotel, it is perched at the top of Quebec City in a spectacular location, and is truly impressive.

Churchill wanted to share Wingate's special type of insurgency with the British and American chiefs of staff. Wingate had built up quite a military reputation and Churchill knew that Roosevelt liked to meet great soldiers, so to cap it all Orde Wingate and his wife met Roosevelt whilst at the conference.

Churchill instinctively arranged for Mrs. Wingate to board the train as a surprise for both of them without giving it too much consideration. Undoubtedly, this would have left a lasting impression with Wingate, his wife, and everyone who knew them. Wingate no doubt would have told his fellow soldiers who in turn would have spread the story until very soon half the army would have heard it. This must have improved morale by proving that whilst Churchill had the weight of the war on his shoulders, he still had time to do something exceptional for a soldier.

Another famous war hero of the time who went along to meet Roosevelt at the same conference was Guy Gibson, the squadron leader of the Dam busters. He was fresh from leading the bouncing bomb attack that famously destroyed the Mohne and Eder Dams.

A further example of Churchill's consideration for others came just after the D-Day landings, when he travelled to France, quite close to the fighting front. He was on a tour of the different battalions and had stopped for lunch. After the break, he got back into his Jeep to see another area of fighting, when his personal body guard realized he hadn't brought a gun for Churchill, a precaution in case they came under attack. The bodyguard took the drivers gun and gave it to Churchill. Churchill then angrily turned to his bodyguard and said, "If I have the driver's gun, what is he going to use if we come under fire." The bodyguard looked at him sheepishly. Churchill gave the driver back his gun and told him to carry on driving, stating that he would take his chances if they were ambushed.

You can guarantee that the whole army on the front would have known of this incident within a couple of days, again demonstrating that Churchill treated everyone equally and would not dream of putting an ordinary soldier in danger for the sake of himself.

As for myself, I cannot think of anything truly exceptional that I have done for those who have worked for me. However, I always go out of my way to demonstrate that I take their wellbeing seriously and that I do not take anything for granted.

I respect their personal time and try not to contact them out of business hours, unless it is a dire emergency. At Christmas, I send a personal card thanking them for their hard work, at least their families then know how much their work is appreciated. If they are involved in an issue within work, they know they can count on my support, so long as they have not broken any major company rules.

If they are having a bad day they can talk to me, I will listen and try to help if possible.

I go out of my way to praise genuine success but do not use it falsely.

During my time at one business, I had been working with a lady in product development to launch a new service; she had been very helpful and did an excellent job despite some major difficulties. When she left to have a baby, I asked my wife to write down a list of items that a first time mum would find useful, and bought her a baby-changing bag filled with baby essentials. I guarantee, just about everyone in product development would have known about my gift. It was just a genuine thank you for all her hard work. I didn't tell any of my colleagues about it at the time, but looking back now, without realizing it, my gift must have helped my profile with others in the product team, which was no bad thing.

When a person is not doing what they are supposed to or I feel is taking advantage, I am very firm and feel quite comfortable confronting a situation that needs resolving. It is especially true in sales; if someone is not performing you do not let them hide behind the myriad of excuses which can be generated by a salesperson. You offer an honest, if sometimes uncomfortable appraisal of the situation. As with other chapters, it is not necessary to do extraordinary deeds all the time for people to know that they matter. Whilst the odd one helps, the manner in which the smallest issue is dealt with and the interaction with other people when help is required can quickly give a measure of your attitude to others.

Churchill understood that doing something extra special for someone as and when the right opportunity arose, would generate immense loyalty. The good deed would gain a life of its own and be a force for good. It can also bring a great deal of personal satisfaction to do someone a good turn.

As an incredibly sad footnote to the story of Major General Wingate, unfortunately towards the end of the war his plane crashed into mountains on the way back to the Far East. I was devastated when I read this, as was Churchill when he was informed. Like so many other war heroes, Orde Wingate was denied the opportunity to enjoy his well-deserved fame.

Chapter 11

Keep Concentration in Compartments

If there is too much going on to cope with, how on earth can you get things done, whilst worrying about the things that there just isn't time for.

How is it possible for concentration to be retained during a discussion or meeting, when a world of worries are competing for a limited amount of attention?

Churchill has to be one of the best examples of someone who had too much on his plate, and yet he managed to attend meeting after meeting, focusing clearly on the content. He prepared hundreds of speeches and wrote thousands of telegrams. Churchill had developed the skill of compartmentalizing an event or task. If he was dictating to a secretary, he gave it his full attention and blocked everything else out of his mind. If he was in a meeting, he was what training consultants often refer to as being "in the moment." He just gave it his full concentration before moving on to the next task.

Examples shown below detail the habits of those who are probably not compartmentalizing. If the answer is yes to any of these questions whist in a conversation or during a meeting then compartmentalizing is not taking place, either at all or not very effectively.

When someone begins speaking, do you immediately start to think of a response before listening completely to the remainder of the conversation?

Do you start thinking of other things whilst giving the appearance of listening to someone talking?

Do you interrupt someone with the suggestion of a solution before the person has even finished speaking?

If you are in a group conversation, as soon as you have something to say, do you stop listening to the rest of the discussion and concentrate on getting your point across?

Do you finish other people's sentences for them when they hesitate?

Do you find it difficult to focus on what someone is saying when you have something on your mind?

Do you often interrupt other people whilst they are talking?

Do you ever keep talking after you have interrupted someone, until the other person stops?

Personally, I probably do one or other of the above regularly, although at least now I am conscious that I do it, which is the first step on the road to stopping.

People who do not compartmentalize generally do one or other of the above. I once worked with a person who could answer yes to the questions above in nearly every meeting, much to the frustration of colleagues.

Compartmentalizing enables a person to be effective at whatever they are doing. Colleagues, staff and customers really appreciate it, as they will feel that they have your individual attention. By not needing things repeated, a quicker more effective response is possible, freeing up time to get on with the next task.

Failure to compartmentalize can lead to stress and anxiety as dealing with a mass of things at the same time becomes almost impossible. The first step to compartmentalizing is beginning to consciously think about doing it when things get very busy. I would describe myself as someone who actively has to think about compartmentalizing in order to achieve it. It does not come that naturally to me. The more I practice, the better I am able to deal with the events of the day and the easier it becomes.

Late one Friday afternoon one of my team called me in considerable distress, she had just been given a major issue to deal with by a customer and was desperate to share it with me. If she had waited until Monday, she knew that it would have been on her mind constantly over the weekend. She was confident that sharing the problem with me wouldn't spoil my weekend as I would be able to forget about it until Monday when it could be resolved. We joked about what she perceived as my ability to do this.

As with any business suggestion, what works for one person might not have any benefit for someone else. The scope of this book is to give a flavor of how Churchill achieved what he did during the war and apply it to a modern context. This book is not a complete guide to everything in business and if a reader can take one thing away that helps to improve their business performance, then (hopefully) it has been worth the price.

Without Churchill's incredible talent to compartmentalize the hundreds of pressing matters that landed on his desk every day, he would not have been as effective. I read that Bill Clinton has an incredible ability to do the same thing. Compartmentalizing is one of the foundation stones of successful people.

There are books' covering every facet of business and there is bound to be one that covers the topic of compartmentalizing more thoroughly and effectively than this chapter. I hope that I have managed to communicate the general principle.

Chapter 12

Praise and Entertain

Churchill was an incredibly charismatic man. He had a fantastically sharp wit. When he was in company, he would always add a splash of humor or witty comment to the proceedings.

If he wrote a telegram, where appropriate he would endeavor to make it interesting for the reader. Churchill was a fantastic writer. By the time he became Prime Minister, he had published numerous books; he was a naturally talented writer. His book "My Early Life" written in 1930, is a cracking read and thought to be one of the greatest biographies of the last century.

Churchill was a great believer in seeking out ways to praise those who deserved it. Not like someone who says everything is fantastic but then no-one believes them when a genuine reason for praise presents itself. If Churchill gave somebody praise, they deserved it and they could be rightly proud. In the memoirs there are numerous examples of notes sent to all manner of people, both civilian and military, praising them and their staff or troops through good times and bad.

Part of Churchill's appeal was his ability to make interaction with him a rewarding experience, for those privileged enough to have the opportunity.

Because of his talent for compartmentalizing he had the ability to make those who worked for him feel special.

This was particularly useful when he was dealing with other world leaders and people he needed to influence to help the war effort. The force of his personality, along with the focus that he could shine upon a person, must have intoxicated anyone trying to stand up to him or refuse a request. It is difficult to imagine sitting in front of Churchill, attempting to say no to a request, once he had empathized with a situation then asked again for its completion. It would have taken some doing.

Having the ability to influence people and achieve results by making them feel special is a great talent. Demonstrating an understanding of issues, whilst asking someone to do something for you, can help get things done both in business and personally.

With modern day communications, the most likely forms of communication are phone, e-mail, videoconferencing and face-to-face meetings. Gone are the days of sending telegrams as the main form of communication. The value of face-to-face meetings, despite the growth in video conferencing, is still just as high as it was in Churchill's day. You just cannot extend the personal touch needed for those important meetings via a video conference.

Normally I tend to do a lot of business over the phone, both with customers and within the company I am working for. Whilst I probably have as much charisma and personality as Churchill had in his big toe, I have found that by endeavoring where possible to make any interaction rewarding for the other person, they are more willing to help. I covered the aspect of treating people decently in an earlier chapter; entertaining them for a few seconds is just going that one-step further towards greater effectiveness.

It can be as simple as asking someone how they are, listening to the answer and making a pleasant comment. Before making a request, recognize that they are probably already very busy and the last thing they need is more work. Make the request. A good line that gets to the nub of when they can complete the task, without being too direct, is to ask how big their to-do list is. Even if they do not have one, they will get the meaning in the question.

If something needs doing urgently, explain why and what the

personal and business benefit would be. This will help them justify to themselves why the request is so important and help them to prioritize it. Refrain from asking for every request to be urgent, as this will damage that all-important credibility.

Even if they state that they cannot give preferential treatment, always finish the call by thanking them anyway, express appreciation for the difficult situation that asking for a priority request has placed them in. It is amazing how often the request completes early, as if by magic.

The above is just one small example of how planning a call of any nature and making the effort to be pleasant, and where appropriate, entertaining can make a real difference. A humorous observation or a joke at your own expense, which often seems to work well, can break the ice before making a request.

The approach on the phone can work equally well on e-mail and face to face, it just takes a little more thought than a phone call.

Obviously, this approach is only suitable in certain situations; it works if the other person has a sense of humor and will not take offence if someone appears to be a bit familiar. Occasionally that happens and I can feel myself crash and burn, which is very embarrassing.

It is important to compartmentalize a conversation, as this enables the other person to feel some sincerity. Avoid feigning sincerity as it requires great skill; it is very easy to see through a fake. When someone is caught faking sincerity, it can cause a great deal of damage. Better to just stick to the facts and not try to entertain.

Churchill had been a politician for forty years before the war started. His had finely tuned his skills of communication and persuasion during his decades spent in government and parliament. Trying to emulate a small fraction of his entertaining ability is not for everyone, it requires a certain type of personality.

Everybody, no matter who they are, can follow the basic principles of courteous communication, which in itself can make a big difference to a person's business effectiveness.

Chapter 13

Survival of the Freshest

The first volume of Churchill's WWII memoirs, (The Gathering Storm) detailed the build up to the War, and why in his view, it should never have happened. Throughout the book it is clear that even though he was over sixty years old, he did not view age as an inhibitor to acquiring knowledge. He was determined to keep up to date with the very latest in military technology, he regularly wrote to the ministers responsible for the Army, Navy, Air force and Home Defense both to check on what they were up to and to make suggestions based on his own extensive military knowledge.

He kept up to date by inviting eminent engineers and professors to his home, Chartwell, grilling them about the latest military developments in Britain and in Germany. Even though he was not a minister, he managed to place himself on a number of government committees, dealing with the research and development of new weapons that would ultimately save Britain from the Germans.

It is worth pointing out that the British National Trust superbly manage Chartwell, they celebrate and preserve Churchill's legacy. It is a truly great day out. I cannot recommend it highly enough.

In Churchill's own words he was not a great technical wizard; he instinctively knew what would help, what would hurt, what would cure and what would kill. He also relied heavily on a chap called Professor Lindeman who he refers to in the books as "the Prof", an eminent scientist who stayed with him throughout the war. The Prof was invaluable to Churchill; he had the extremely useful talent of being able to translate the most complex technical detail into plain English.

Churchill was convinced that without British invention and ingenuity the war could well have been lost.

A couple of examples of the critical inventions the British were developing before the war were RDF (Radio Detection Finding) as it was known in 1935 and ASDICS (Anti Submarine Detection Investigation Committee). Without these fantastic military aids, Britain in the dark days of 1940 standing alone against the might of the German threat, would have been at the most severe disadvantage. RDF is now in use everywhere and today it is widely known as RADAR.

Churchill readily acknowledged that whilst the British scientist Professor Appleton was developing RADAR, the Germans were also developing the same technology. In 1939, the Germans sent the Graff Zeppelin airship along the south coast of Britain with RADAR detection equipment, trying to discover if Britain had effective RADAR defenses. The Germans wanted to discover the locations of Britain's RADAR transmitters. Britain in 1939 had the most sophisticated air defense system in the world. The Germans had their spies and probably knew that Britain had developed and implemented RADAR. Unfortunately, for the Germans, on the day of the flight, the Zeppelin air ship's detection equipment did not function properly. It was a year later that this fantastic achievement of British science and engineering was pivotal in determining the future direction of the free world.

Both sides at this stage had RADAR; the real difference was how Britain had implemented it. At the height of the Battle of Britain, this was one of the key factors in stopping the Germans gaining air superiority. The British had RADAR stations all around the coast, which could detect enemy aircraft at a range of sixty miles. The other key to the practical application of RADAR was IFF (Identification Friend or Foe) without which you could not tell at 60 miles if a plane was British or German.

The British, unlike the Germans had linked all the RADAR stations back to Royal Air Force Fighter Command in Uxbridge using thousands of miles of "telephonic communication wire", effectively creating the first integrated defense network in the world. In addition, fifty thousand people from the observer corps had phones linking them back to central command. They watched the sky and reported on all plane activities. All of this information was transmitted back to hundreds of people working in fighter command, who then assessed it. The end result was a huge board, the size of a cinema screen, with different colored light bulbs signifying when planes were in the air, under attack or in reserve. All this communication gave central fighter command up to the minute knowledge of what was happening in the air at any given time. It was far in advance of any other defense network at that time.

The practical manner in which RADAR was implemented made all the difference. Fighter Command could detect the Germans coming and scramble fighters to intercept them. This control from one central point meant that the British could make the best use of available fighters. Without the invention and application of RADAR, the thousand or so fighter pilots who saved the world from German domination, as mentioned in an earlier chapter, might well have failed in their task.

RADAR development was quickly expanded to include the control of searchlights and anti aircraft guns. On ships, it helped detect the enemy from far away and enabled shelling to take place accurately, from a long distance. Planes used it for locating German submarines as they resurfaced to recharge their batteries. RADAR must be one of the greatest inventions of all time, based on the simple fact that Britain could well have lost the war without it.

ASDICS was another truly important British invention, at the outset of war it was in active service. It was developed to detect and destroy submarines and is known today as SONAR. Having survived the Battle of Britain and embarrassed the Luftwaffe the next task was to survive the Battle of the Atlantic.

Britain shared all this advanced technology with America; it was in Britain's interest for its Allies to receive equal protection. The Americans took the research and with their considerable pool of talented scientists and money, helped refine it, and then gave it back to Britain.

Throughout the war Hitler was forever promising his Commanders that the latest and greatest German invention would lead to Britain's downfall. The first example of this was the magnetic mine; deployed early in 1940 it had a devastating effect on shipping around the Channel coast. Previously, mines would only detonate when a boat hit them; the magnetic mine would detonate when the metal hull of a ship passed nearby. Initially, the British had no answer to this devastating new weapon, it took a number of months and some incredible good luck to come up with the solution.

An observer noticed a plane dropping what looked like mines off the coast of Southend, along the east coast of England. By chance, the mines landed in soft sand. A bomb disposal team went out to recover them.

The team took two perilous days to defuse the mines. It was worth all the effort and risk, as at the end of the process they recovered two magnetic mines, intact. The defense research teams then went to work on devising a solution to the threat posed by this new and deadly weapon. The problem was resolved by degaussing all the ships. Degaussing for those that do not know, and I certainly did not before reading Churchill's books, is as follows; the hull of a ship would have electric wire wrapped around it and an electric current passed through the wire, this then offset the magnetic effect of the ship, effectively de-magnetizing it. Once the solution became clear, a huge project quickly degaussed just about every essential ship in the Navy and Merchant Navy within three months, rendering the magnetic mines ineffective.

On the subject of bomb disposal teams, one particular team nicknamed the Holy Trinity, receives special mention in Churchill's memoirs and illustrates how all the British social classes of the time joined in during the war. The Holy Trinity consisted of The Earl of Suffolk, his seventy-year-old chauffeur and his young personal secretary. They built up a reputation for survival because they successfully defused thirty-four bombs, saving hundreds of lives in the process. Sadly, the thirty-fifth bomb got them. I do not know what the average survival rate was for a bomb disposal team during the war but this must have been an heroic effort.

There were many difficult wartime jobs but few had more certainty of death than that of a bomb disposal expert. Bomber and fighter pilots had it tough. Being a soldier was a hazardous business. A sailor in the Navy was always in danger of a torpedo attack by a German sub. At least the three main services had the potential to fight back to a greater or lesser extent.

It is impossible and unfair to compare the bravery of the men and women in the services however, special mention must go to those unsung heroes, the sailors of the Merchant Navy. It must have been the most unnerving experience, sailing across the Atlantic knowing that your ship could be sunk at any time, never knowing when it might happen, and incapable of defending the ship from the U-Boat menace.

In the early part of the war shipping losses were measured in hundreds of thousands of tons, on a monthly basis. At the peak of the Battle of the Atlantic, it was common to have fifteen to twenty ships sunk out of a convoy of thirty. One convoy going to Archangel in Russia had only four ships arrive out of a convoy of twenty-nine. All the sailors died in the freezing cold waters of the Barents Sea. In 1940, the worst year, two and a half million tons of supplies sank, comprising hundreds of ships and countless sailors.

The Battle of the Atlantic started in 1940; it was effectively Britain battling to survive the threat from German U boats, whilst trying desperately to get enough weapons, food and materials across the Atlantic to feed the British people and take the fight to Hitler. As well as facing a threat from beneath the waves, merchant ships faced an equally deadly hazard from long-range bombers.

One early method of defense against the bombers was to catapult a single fighter plane from a merchant ship. This could be in the middle of the Atlantic Ocean with the plane unable to land back on the ship. The pilot would attack the bomber and would then have to eject from the plane, as near to the merchant ship as possible. Hopefully, the crew would then fish him out of the water. It must have taken a seriously brave man to undertake such a mission.

Churchill was unable to mention in his memoirs a key factor in how Britain won the Battle of the Atlantic; it was still top secret when he was writing them. The finest mathematical minds based at Bletchley, in the south of England received a German Enigma machine retrieved from a sunken U-Boat. They managed after many months to crack the code. The Enigma machine communicated the positions of the German submarines back to the admiralty. With such vital information the British and American Navy were able to hunt down and sink the subs considerably reducing their affect.

From an early age technology has always been a source of great fascination to me, forming the basis of a career which I dropped in favor of sales at the age of twenty-five. My technical background bred a natural curiosity to uncover the latest advances in technology affecting whatever products or services were in my sales portfolio. Whist in sales role number one, selling photocopiers, change was rapid, copiers evolved from optical to digital, from black and white to color, from standalone to networked.

In 1988 after many weeks of residential training, the company I was working for at the time added a radical new product to the portfolio of copiers and faxes; it was the forerunner of Windows. This system had a huge black and white screen with icons for documents. Printing a customer proposal simply required the dragging of a document icon across the screen onto a printer icon using a mouse, a box would pop up requesting the required number of prints, then a high quality printout would appear from a networked laser printer in the middle of the office. Pretty standard now, but state of the art in 1988; considerably better than the tiny little things Apple then produced and years ahead of Windows. Incidentally, a large number of the team responsible for its development ended up working for both Apple and Microsoft!

These big document systems cost an absolute fortune. In 1989 a colleague demonstrated Windows, which, including an IBM PC cost about a sixth of its price. Windows at the time was not nearly as advanced, but was rapidly evolving, and quickly developed similar functionality to the large systems we offered. Sales of the large systems dried up rapidly. Looking back now it is clear that the mistake my company made was insisting on selling the software with the hardware and printers. Seeing it only as means of helping to sell additional equipment and not developing it to work on other platforms. Bill Gates took a different approach, concentrating on the software and leaving the hardware to anyone that could make and sell it, clearly not a bad idea, given that he has done pretty well since 1989.

Had the copier company had the foresight to develop the software to work on PC based platforms and not been so fixated on selling the hardware, they might well have given Windows a run for its money in the early days.

The copier company consisted mainly of older guys (about my age now) who were used to selling in a certain way and who had been very successful in the past. The world was changing and the old guys were determined to stick to the same routines as long as they could. They were only too happy to quote how much money they had earned a few years ago, bemoaning how the market had changed and how it was everybody else's fault but their own. These people had not adapted to the changing marketplace and struggled to survive in the new technological world. A fate that will hopefully not befall yours truly.

During three different careers, across eight different businesses, the one constant is that about every two years large-scale changes have taken effect; the result of advances in computer technology, making things faster, smaller, cheaper and more or less complex depending on the application.

This technology change has been among the most dramatic in the telecoms industry. Ten years ago, a new area of business was developed called Minutes Reselling, where intermediary companies sold phone calls to businesses. Instead of businesses buying their calls from someone like British Telecom in Britain, they would buy them from a reseller. The reseller would then use an alternative network provider who would route the calls at a lower cost and provide them with the information needed to produce a bill and make a profit. Many resellers became very successful offering this service, whilst reducing their client's phone bills. They now face a major problem. The industry is on the edge of a major technological change that will dramatically alter how they do business and make money.

Without getting too technical, in a few years time businesses will not use existing telephone systems to make phone calls; they will use a number of different types of internet and specialist data connections (referred to as internet voice services for the balance of this chapter). Instead of having a phone system in the office, many end users will have all the functionality of the phone system provided for them via the internet.

A significant proportion of the resellers currently selling the old voice services are hoping that this new type of business will just go away, leaving them to carry on happily with business as usual. It will not!

The resellers are taking the same approach as Germany's neighbors did seventy years ago, hoping that the problem will just miraculously pass them by. Whilst the consequences will not be as drastic, they are at the point the world was in 1935. Concerted action then could have prevented war, just as preparation and planning now, could save a resellers business in the long run.

I had a meeting with the owners of a typical reseller, both very nice people who have a great business that runs very efficiently, they offer their customers a good service. By partnering with the right sort of suppliers they should be able to adapt to the changing world of voice services over the internet. However, this is by no means certain. In order to survive they will need to make big changes to their whole business and even then, there is no guarantee of success. The market is going to change so completely in the next few years, that there is no absolute guarantee any of the current resellers will be able to adapt. As Germany's neighbors found out, sometimes planning and preparation will not save you, when faced with a brand new unquantifiable threat.

Many businesses have decided that with the uncertain future ahead, it may be beneficial to cash in and sell up. For some of the resellers this is the right decision however, others may be undervaluing their business, as I believe that resellers with the right types of customer could potentially prosper as the market changes.

There is no such thing as a job for life, a technology for life, or a business for life. Staying fresh and in tune with new techniques and technology, adapting to everything that is going on around is what Churchill did before the war. However sometimes a business does not, or cannot, adapt in time to new external market forces and goes bust.

My second sales job was working for a company selling computer aided microfilm retrieval systems. The year before I joined, they had their best year ever. Not long after starting, it became clear to me that the market was on the brink of a major change. People no longer wanted microfilm, they wanted digital storage on CD disks. The microfilm company did not have this technology; it was only a matter of time before a new job was required. Luckily, the recruitment agent used for the microfilm job found a position with a major brand, selling printers to large corporations, in the days when printers were as expensive as computers. Four enjoyable years ensued, working for a great manager called Jon Alexander. Eventually there was so little profit left in printers that before it was too late another move was required.

Throughout a long sales career, every year I have always found it useful to carry out a personal audit of the current employer and the general state of the business environment. When it has been clear that the market place was in the process of changing, using personal experience, I would form a view of how successfully my present employer would adapt to the new market conditions. A conclusion that pointed to the downsizing of the business would see a new role sought elsewhere.

No matter how clever or how good someone is at his or her present job, inevitably the world keeps travelling along a road of progress. Once the quest to keep up with the latest advances in techniques and technology stops, people start going backwards, as the world starts to pass them by.

Before Churchill took charge of the Admiralty and re-joined the government at the outset of war, he had been out of favor with his own party and significant sections of parliament. He kept up to date with the latest military technologies, and was aware of the devastating consequences the new weapons of war would bring. He tried to warn his colleagues, but received ferocious criticism and was labeled a warmonger. Despite this he persisted in his quest for knowledge. For Churchill even at the age of sixty-five staying fresh was a matter of life and death.

Chapter 14

Success is Happily Finding Your Level

Churchill would find one particular aspect of today's society very puzzling. Celebrity culture, the difference between those who achieve success and become famous as a result, and those who are famous without any substance.

In Churchill's day, widespread recognition was earned due to achievement. Fame would follow on from success in fields such as acting, sport, politics, science, business etc.

Celebrity was not an ambition in itself in the way it appears to be today. There wasn't the voracious demand in the old days to fill TV channels with a recognizable face, even if they were only famous for being filmed going about their daily lives. TV did not exist and neither did the whole madness of those who desperately try to achieve public recognition. The list goes on of the different angles that have been used to achieve a sufficient public profile to make a living. Not all the reality TV shows have been bad, (the ground breaking Osbournes was excellent) neither are all the talent shows, but in my opinion the vast majority are total rubbish.

A few lucky people with no obvious talent other than being their quirky cheeky selves have succeeded in making millions as a result of appearing on a reality TV show. Somehow they have connected with the public for a short while by doing no more than being themselves. I am not criticizing those who have succeeded or the many that have tried. A willing public will have its fill and then move on to something else. The problem is that they add to the perception that you can make money and be a success without actually doing anything other than being in the right place at the right time.

With so many reality TV shows available it is difficult to keep up. Whilst I will catch the odd one, I particularly dislike the fly-on-the-wall shows following the lives of celebrities who only achieved fame by appearing on a reality show in the first place. The desperation of some TV channels for programming is breathtaking.

A chapter dealing with the harsh reality that the vast majority of successful people happen to be that way because they are more intelligent or have worked hard for their success is at odds with the expectations of a large section of the population. There are plenty of books promising to help a person achieve wealth and happiness by taking shortcuts, and a big enough audience sufficiently gullible to buy them.

I know quite a few very rich, successful people who have made millions by having an idea and working incredibly hard to make it a success. Some of them would not necessarily be called naturally intelligent, by any IQ test measurement. The common trait in all the successful people I know is an exceptionally high degree of will power. This helped overcome the problems associated with turning an idea into a success.

Churchill would recognize this trait; his final report from school gave no hint of the greatness he was to achieve, marking him out as someone who could aspire to mediocrity. What he had which leaps out from the pages of his memoirs, was an unfailing will to succeed, married with an abundance of self-belief. History had taught him that the side with the greater will to win had gained all the great victories in evenly matched battles. This inner strength stopped him succumbing to the pressure from his war cabinet, when on the 26th May 1940 Lord Halifax, the most senior government figure at the time, attempted to persuade Churchill and the other senior ministers to negotiate terms with Hitler, before the inevitable fall of France.

Nobody expected the miracle of Dunkirk; the optimistic predictions envisaged that thirty thousand troops would escape from French soil. Halifax correctly argued that Britain would be able to negotiate better terms with Hitler before the French capitulated. The cabinet took these proposals very seriously; over three days, nine meetings took place. Churchill at this point was new to the job of Prime Minister and was in a relatively weak position politically. If he had not persuaded the cabinet to fight on, then resignation would have been his only option, leaving peace negotiations to Halifax. It was touch and go right up to the last meeting, with the war cabinet split evenly on what was to be the most important decision they ever made. Halifax was actively trying to convince the waverers that Britain stood little chance against the might of the Nazi's, and would be better off doing a deal with Hitler.

Modern history has been hard on the French for surrendering to the Nazi's. I shared this view until I read Churchill's memoirs; the French stood no chance against the incredibly sophisticated and organized German war machine. Many hundreds of thousands of brave French troops died trying to defend their homeland from a hated invader. Many thousands more suffered to resist the occupation. In the end the French made the same decision I believe the British would have eventually had to take, with all the potential consequences for the world, and which by so thin a margin was avoided in the summer of 1940. The French fought the Germans on their own soil; Halifax was all for a negotiated settlement without a single German jackboot setting foot in Britain.

Quick anecdote, I was in a bar and during a discussion, an American man stated that George Bush was responsible for the very funny but unfair line about the French of "cheese eating surrender monkeys" which was prominent during the build up to the Iraq invasion. He was most upset when I pointed out to him that Homer Simpson was in fact responsible for the immortal line!

If Churchill had not won the argument there would have been no Battle of Britain, no D-Day, and the outlook for America would have been bleak (as described in an earlier chapter). Despite trying to convince Halifax personally on a number of occasions, he would not budge from his position.

Churchill then pulled a brilliant masterstroke; he called a meeting of the full cabinet and explained the position. He finished his presentation by stating that if the story of Great Britain was to come to an end, after a thousand years when countless millions had died throughout centuries of war protecting British freedom, such a heritage demanded that Britain go down fighting. The Nazi's would have to fight for every square foot of British soil if they wanted to dominate Europe. The cabinet all cheered him and rushed up to pat him on the back. When he went again to the war cabinet, and told them of the extraordinary reaction of their colleagues, the war cabinet unanimously united behind him leaving Halifax isolated. He knew he had lost the argument and the topic never surfaced again.

Churchill never mentioned this crucial episode in his memoirs as some of the people involved were still alive when they were published. It was some years later when cabinet papers were released that the magnitude of his achievement became widely known.

There can be few greater examples of one persons will power making such a difference to the history of the world.

Churchill would not recognize modern society's singular desire to measure a person's achievement by the amount of money they have. These days, to be considered successful you have to be rich or famous and preferably both. Using this restricted definition, only those who have plenty of money can be considered a success.

For an Army to win a battle requires soldiers, along with a chain of command back to the Generals making the decisions. Without the hard work, dedication and fighting spirit of the soldier the battle would be lost. A Country needs people whose ambition is to be a soldier, an army could not take the fight to the enemy, if everyone wanted to be an officer.

If a regular business task is boring or mundane, then employing someone who is good at it and happy to complete it ensures a job well done. Not everyone is ambitious and wants to be in charge of a business or to manage people. Successful organizations manage to motivate all staff, to consistently and willingly perform to a high standard, regardless of the job or function.

There are occasions when working with someone clever and ambitious is a benefit and times when they cannot add value. If I were trapped in a jungle surrounded by people wishing to do me harm I would prefer to be at the side of someone who was good with a gun, the only thing that would matter would be their survival skills and their ability to help me out of the predicament.

Success is a relative measurement. Someone will always be richer or poorer, a better writer, (definitely in my case), a more accomplished singer or musician, greater at sport or brighter academically, the list goes on. Comparing success against a group of peers can be useful; however, the true measurement can only come from within, when someone happily finds their level in life.

A good friend of mine, Pete, who has sadly passed away was a truck driver; he took great pride in always completing his food deliveries on time. He went on to become an accomplished sewage disposal engineer. Pete would delight in describing some of the dangers associated with emptying industrial cesspits, a real example of someone who loved his job.

Bobby, another good friend of mine, is an expert JCB operator who works in Bermuda. He is an artist with a digger; if you want a complex shape cutting out of the earth Bobby is your man. He takes great pride in his work and is dedicated to doing the best job possible; people such as Bobby build walls, erect buildings, lay roads and sculpture gardens; without such people, none of these things would be possible. Bobby enjoys his job, but struggles with the cost of living in Bermuda and is re-locating to Canada were he plans to continue in the construction business.

While touching the subject of Canada, it is worth pointing out that the Canadians were one of the first countries to support Britain in the war; they committed soldiers long before Pearl Harbor brought America into the conflict.

No matter how rich or successful you are, when a plumber is needed to clear the drains or unblock a toilet, you quickly realize that in the same way as an air force needs everyone from pilots to windshield cleaners, the world only functions when people are prepared to do a job. It functions better when the people doing the job are happy to do it and can do the job successfully.

A successful parking attendant might be someone who fairly gives out tickets to those who deserve it, meeting targets, while showing a bit of leniency on occasion. (Never met one but I live in hope). If a street sweeper has overcome great personal or physical problems to allow them to sweep streets, then who is to say that by their own measurement they are not a success.

A mum or dad in today's society, who gives up a career to run a house and raise children, whilst supporting a partner, is not recognized. Raising and supporting a well-balanced family is one of the most important jobs; it contributes massively to the partner out earning the money and helps children to grow up and achieve their full potential, building the society of the future. How can that not be a successful job? Churchill who was married for over sixty years would not have achieved greatness without the support of his wife Clementine.

My wife has a friend, an accountant who is divorced; she has worked exceptionally hard to support her two daughters and now has a very well paid job, jetting all over the world. Clearly, a success, because she overcame adversity and now earns lots of money. A friend of mine's sister had a child with a guy who it turned out was married and spent years on income support as a single mother. Not content with her situation she took a drop in benefits and got a job as a teaching assistant at a local school. She went back to college to train as a special needs teacher and now has a well-paid job helping young kids with learning difficulties. A success because she overcame even greater adversity and now earns a lot more money than she would have done on benefits. She would not be considered a success by society's monetary measurement, but who cares! Both these women may not be finished with their careers, however, it is hard to argue that they have not each worked hard to achieve great success in their respective lives.

There is nothing wrong with a person being the best they can be to the limit of their ability, ambition and will power. Without the millions of people who are willing to do jobs at all levels, the world would just not function.

Churchill came from an elitist background; he was a descendent of John Churchill, the Duke of Marlborough, one of Britain's greatest military commanders (son of the first Sir Winston Churchill), who two hundred and forty years before had led an army of European allies to victory over the French army of Louis XIV. Saving Britain and Europe from a tyrant who wanted to impose his regime upon the free world, (Sound familiar?). Churchill was also half-American and could trace his ancestors on his mother's side back to an officer who fought against the British in the war of Independence.

With such a rich heritage Churchill must have felt great satisfaction when in 1950, the Queen offered him a similar Dukedom to that of his great ancestor and hero (Which he declined). It would be an understatement to say that Winston added to the illustrious family name.

Despite his background, he knew that in order to win the war it would require everyone across society to work hard for victory. He valued the munitions workers and the dockers, the farmers and the laborers equally, without everyone pulling together success would have been impossible. One of those he singles out for special praise in his memoirs is a chap called Lord Leathers who coordinated the entire commercial and military shipping throughout the war. He never lifted a gun against the enemy however Churchill was convinced that he was crucial to the successful prosecution of the war.

Chapter 15

Don't be Afraid to Coldly Comprehend

Throughout the war, there are countless people, from Hitler downwards, who Churchill could have simply contented himself with despising because of who they were, what they did, or what they stood for. It would have taken a brave person to calmly explain why Hitler became such a tyrant and treated people so appallingly, but that is exactly what Churchill did in his book. Time and again, he would provide an overview of the reasons why he believed other wicked people throughout the war behaved in a certain fashion. He did this in a matter of fact way that did not seek to make any excuses for these people, just to place before the reader the facts as he saw them. He took the time to comprehend his enemy.

The word comprehend is deliberately used instead of understand. To understand might imply a certain sympathy or agreement with a person. To comprehend something allows assimilation of information whilst remaining completely dispassionate about it.

Comprehending a person might have no influence whatsoever on how you deal with them. In the case of Hitler, Churchill explained that towards the end of WWI, Hitler was blinded in action temporarily. He was recuperating in hospital when Germany admitted defeat and signed the armistice. Hitler could not understand why this happened, eventually convincing himself that German Jews had somehow betrayed the German nation by forcing them to capitulate. He blamed them for his failure to get a job as an artist and for the poverty and hardship Germany suffered after the war. When he rose to power by ruthlessly manipulating and killing his opponents, he used the Jews as an excuse for everything. The German people at the time bought into this fiction, blinded by Hitler's charisma and lies.

Churchill's memoirs surprisingly make no mention of the holocaust and the horrors perpetrated on the Jewish people by Hitler. It could possibly be due to the sensitivity of the subject, that he felt unable to tackle it. Once Churchill had coldly comprehend Hitler's motivations, he devoted himself from the early 1930's to try and force Britain to re-arm in anticipation of what he correctly predicted was an inevitable war. He then used everything in his power to defeat Hitler. Churchill, even though he had a comprehension of Hitler, judged him by his actions, which were wicked and despicable. He treated him accordingly.

To coldly comprehend, is to judge a person or a situation by what actions have taken place or are planned, or by how someone treats others, disregarding their motivation or background story. This approach prevents prior knowledge or personal information from clouding an opinion or decision.

Churchill almost had dinner with Hitler in 1930. He was in Germany researching the locations of his ancestor the Duke of Marlborough's great battles. In particular Blenheim, the location of his most famous victory and the name given to the huge palace built for the Duke by a grateful nation, at huge cost three hundred and fifty years ago. If you ever get the chance to visit Blenheim Palace I would recommend it. It is a truly great stately home, brilliantly run by the current Duke.

A personal assistant to Hitler, befriended Churchill whilst he was staying at the best hotel in Munich. This was of course no accident. Hitler was keen to meet the famous Churchill and he was probably trying to size up a potential opponent.

After a few days, the assistant said that Hitler was having dinner the following evening and would like Churchill to join him. At this point Hitler was a well-known figure in Germany who Churchill was aware of; at the time he just thought of him as a patriotic supporter of Germany, keen to see his country climb out of economic depression. Churchill had no great reason to refuse to see Hitler. The assistant joined Churchill for dinner the night before the meeting and they chatted about all manner of topics. Churchill asked the assistant why Hitler hated Jews so much, as it seemed odd that a man could hate a whole race. It was one thing to hate a specific person for something that they had done, however he could not understand how somebody could hate a whole section of society.. The assistant did not offer any answer to Churchill but moved the conversation on to other topics.

The following day the assistant phoned the hotel and advised that Herr Hitler would not be able to make dinner, as something had cropped up. Churchill assumed that the assistant had told him about their conversation and that Hitler no longer wanted to meet him. It is possible that Hitler would have found it uncomfortable, explaining himself to a person of Churchill's stature. Hitler invited Churchill to meet with him many times after Munich, but by then he had started to display some of his well-known tyrannical qualities. As a result, Churchill always refused the meetings.

Churchill also gave a description of Mussolini, someone he had met quite a few times in the twenties and thirties. He believed that Mussolini wanted to restore the Roman Empire to its former glory, and that he chose to fight alongside the Nazi's because Hitler had promised to give him the British and French African territories, without having to spill too much Italian blood. Mussolini viewed it as the opportunity of a thousand years and was determined to grab it. He vainly wanted the fame associated with Italy's great historic emperors. "Ill Duce" achieved fame for all the wrong reasons; his own people hanged him from a street lamppost.

The Japanese had the same opportunistic idea; they saw an opportunity to grab the eastern part of the British and Dutch empire along with large parts of China. Japan correctly calculated that Britain had committed all its resources to the fight with Germany, making it difficult to mount an effective defense of the

British Eastern Empire. Churchill detailed the hard choices he had to make between fighting the Germans in North Africa, sending troops to the Far East, or defending the colonies. Churchill concluded that victory against Germany required the majority of British resources to be focused on Europe. Allied Eastern command would have to make best use of the men and equipment available. Whilst no one admitted it at the time, he sacrificed the Far East to allow the deployment of maximum resources against the Germans.

It was the policy of the British government that if Australia or New Zealand came under direct attack from Japan, they would sacrifice the desert campaign. North African troops would run to the defense of "our kith and kin" as Churchill put it.

The Japanese did such a good job of conquering the British colonies that New Zealand and Australia in particular felt very threatened, despite the logistical impossibility (as Churchill saw it) of a large-scale Japanese invasion. Britain could not offer an absolute guarantee to Australia, so the newly formed labor government demanded that large numbers of troops be withdrawn from the North Africa campaign and sent home. Churchill repeatedly argued that transporting the troops to Australia would put them in mortal danger from enemy attack whilst on board ship. General Alexander complained bitterly about the withdrawal of such high quality troops from the field of battle, eventually the Royal Navy ran great risks to ship the soldiers back. In fairness to the Australians, they supported Britain at the outset of war; their soldiers distinguished themselves in many conflicts, including Greece, Crete and North Africa.

India had such a dislike of Britain six years before independence, that significant factions would have preferred the Japanese to attack. With everything else Churchill had to contend with, India caused him great difficulties. India wanted Britain to grant independence immediately, in return for access to their ports. Britain only wanted access to the ports to defend India from Japanese attack. India's politicians eventually concluded that continuing as part of the British Empire was preferable to life under a Japanese flag. Churchill correctly argued that it would have been impossible to deal with the complex nature of independence whilst fighting a world war. Once it was over India would be granted independence. It took a considerable amount of time and effort to reach agreement with India's politicians, which was an unwanted distraction for Churchill. He balanced his criticism of Indian opportunism, by stating that many thousands of brave Indian soldiers fought and died supporting the war effort in the Far East and Europe.

The Japanese made their big mistake when they decided to attack America. Pearl Harbor not only spelled the doom of Japan but also sealed the fate of Hitler. Japan hugely miscalculated Pearl Harbor's effect on American public opinion. The USA instantly went from opposition to direct involvement in the war, to a desire for retribution upon the nation who committed such a terrible act of aggression. It seems inconceivable that Japan could have been so stupid as to directly attack America and then not expect the mighty American military machine to eventually recover and seek revenge. They clearly underestimated America in the same way that Germany underestimated Britain.

Had Japan limited its greed and concentrated on China along with the British and Dutch colonies, they would probably have been a lot more successful. Without the direct attack, the American public would not have allowed troops to be committed in Europe and Asia to fight and die in someone else's war. Roosevelt in his election campaign of 1940 had stated categorically "your boys will not be sent overseas to war". Without Pearl Harbor, massive amounts of military aid would not have flowed as easily to Russia. It did not do Hitler any favors; he would have had a better chance against a Russian army that was not receiving all the latest military equipment from America and Britain.

Hitler had gone out of his way to avoid conflict with America allowing them to increase support to Britain and in the case of the Atlantic convoys, allowing the US Navy to guard British merchant ships against German U-boat attacks. When the US Navy encountered a U-Boat, they would directly radio its position to a

British sub and if fired upon would retaliate. Germany would have declared war on any other country that committed such acts of aggression; however, Hitler was rightly afraid of entering a war with America whilst he had so many other commitments. As it turned out, with very good reason.

Who can know what would have happened, if Japan had taken a different course. One thing is clear from Churchill's memoirs, all these events are interrelated in a way that it is difficult for the general public to comprehend. What happens on one side of the world can have a direct effect on another military campaign thousands of miles away. Churchill firmly believed that once America came in to the war, it was a matter of when and not if the Germans would be defeated.

Roosevelt must be the best friend Britain has ever had. His close friend Harry Hopkins, who Churchill really admired, passed a private message from Roosevelt to Churchill twelve months before Pearl Harbor. He asked Harry to tell Churchill, "for as long as I live I will not see Britain go down to the Nazi's" and that "Britain's war is America's war". It was just a matter of time before he could convince the American public to send their boys overseas. Roosevelt stayed true to his word, right up to his dying breath, writing letters to Churchill about war matters literally hours before he knew he was going to die. Churchill did not know he was so gravely ill and felt terrible for troubling him when he was in such a bad way. Political leaders were made of strong stuff in those days. One of Churchill's big regrets was that he could not pull himself away from the War to attend Roosevelt's funeral. He stated that if he had his time again, he would have gone.

Churchill does not actually say it in his memoirs, but you can read between the lines that Roosevelt was determined to get America into the war and was convinced that only something dramatic would change public opinion. Roosevelt had only just managed to persuade congress by one vote to bring back the draft; he had no chance of persuading them to vote for war even though he was personally convinced of the need for America to become directly involved. US Intelligence had been able to decipher Japanese radio transmissions long before Pearl Harbor; Churchill thought it inconceivable that someone high up in the US military did not know what was going to happen. He suggests that Roosevelt may have prevented any advanced warnings of the impending attack, encouraging an outraged America to go to war. Roosevelt and his senior advisers knew what could happen if they stood on the sidelines of the European conflict for too much longer. If they did really allow the attack to happen, then they did so in the full knowledge that they were doing the right thing and who can argue that history has proven them correct.

At the time of Pearl Harbor, British nuclear research was far in advance of the USA. If the worst had happened and America had stayed out of the war, after defeating Russia, the Nazi's might have successfully invaded Britain. They could have gained access to Britain's nuclear research. Some years later it might have been a German bomber, flying from an old British aircraft carrier, dropping an Atom Bomb on a US city. Who knows…?

Whilst Roosevelt recognized that Germany should be defeated before Japan, significant factions in the US military were not convinced. Churchill had to work hard to win the argument, writing many letters and sending large military delegations across the Atlantic to argue the position. As was the case right up until the latter part of the war, Winston got what he wanted and the planning began for Operation Overlord, the D Day landings.

It is impossible to comprehend why Japans military treated Allied soldiers so badly, and certainly difficult to put into a few words in the context of this book. According to Churchill, Japanese tradition was to despise anyone who surrendered to an enemy, believing they would have to face their ancestors and be shamed for eternity. They would sooner commit suicide than surrender, preferring what they believed to be an honorable death than a dishonorable life. A westerner would have real difficulty comprehending this attitude to life. If a captured soldier was staring down the barrel of a gun, better to surrender with dignity and try to escape later. At the very least, they would have a chance of seeing their homeland and loved ones again. Western opinion did not see any shame in being a prisoner of war. Because they would not do it themselves, the Japanese had no respect for prisoners who surrendered and dreadfully mistreated them.

It is one thing to comprehend why the Japanese did what they did. This does not mean that there is even the slightest excuse for the way they behaved.

Most businesses have to compete with other companies for contracts. Comprehending what the competition is capable of and trying to get as much information about them is critical. Forming a balanced judgment about how the competition will behave in a given scenario, increases the prospect of winning the business. This is also true when comprehending a customer's business, the better the granularity of knowledge, the greater the likelihood a proposal has of matching the customers needs.

In a service industry, it is vital to have a thorough comprehension of the target customer. Without such knowledge, how is it possible to tailor a service to meet their needs and capture their business?

Regardless of the job or profession, if interaction with people or companies is required, then only good can flow from taking the time to comprehend where people are coming from. To comprehend does not require any sympathy or agreement. As Churchill demonstrated in his books, it simply means better-informed decisions.

Chapter 16

Dealing with the Stalin's of This World

One of the toughest business tasks is to deal with difficult, ungrateful customers. For some, no matter how much hard work takes place on their behalf, they take the attitude that it is never good enough. Constantly expecting more, even when behind the scenes everyone is trying their utmost to help. For some reason companies spend fortunes on training people to negotiate, present and sell, but very little on the subject of dealing with nightmare customers. Over the years through trial and error, you develop some method of coping with these situations. Not all customers are difficult to deal with; it is normally limited to one or two individuals that do their utmost to make life difficult and unpleasant.

The way Churchill dealt with the Soviet Union during the war was like reading a handbook on how to treat this complicated and difficult subject. Since finishing Churchill's memoirs my approach when dealing with such a situation has changed considerably.

In 1939, at the outset of war, Russia under the rule of Stalin was not directly fighting Britain. However, they were actively helping the Germans by providing food, iron ore and other war materials to help defeat the British. Communist backed agitators in Britain tried to make things difficult for the government by spreading anti war propaganda. Stalin regularly denounced Britain in broadcasts and newspaper articles. Russia tried to invade Finland and failed. As Germany conquered more and more of Europe, Stalin pressured the likes of Ukraine and Lithuania to become Soviet satellite states.

When Germany invaded Poland, the Soviet Union took a piece of Poland as part of a deal struck with the Germans.

Up until June 1941, the Soviet Union formed part of the axis of powers ranged against Britain. They wanted Germany to defeat Britain and were looking forward to receiving their share of the British Empire, as a reward for supporting the German war effort.

Hitler was simply following his usual process of trying to defeat one enemy at a time, keeping the next one in line deluded, whilst finishing off his current victim, in this case Britain.

The codename for the campaign against Britain was operation Sea Lion, under such directives, all the planning required to defeat a country was coordinated. For the Russians the codename for the attack was Barbarossa. Hitler gave this order in November 1940, six months before the Germans invaded.

Churchill in his books tried to tell it like it was, sometimes being self-critical and sometimes criticizing others. Considering Russia had become the biggest threat to world peace by the time he wrote his memoirs, he does not spare Stalin, or the rest of the people responsible for Soviet war direction from his honest opinions.

The Germans played the Soviets like a violin, right up to the day before they invaded. Churchill believed Stalin showed himself to be completely inept in his relations with Hitler. Accepting the word of a charismatic man, who had said the same thing, to the last ten countries he had conquered. On the day before the invasion of Russia the Germans used high speed freight trains to get the last of the supplies they could out of Russia, before they declared war. They had amassed the biggest single army the world had ever seen on the Russian front; however, Stalin refused point blank to accept all the warnings given to him by well-informed people.

Churchill made a speech in parliament a few days before the invasion, predicting it would happen. This was widely reported on the night before operation Barbarossa began. Stalin denounced Churchill, and Britain, for attempting to stir up trouble between

Russia and its German allies. Churchill, as a result of Britain's spy network and the ability to decipher German secret communications, actually set aside time to write a speech for a radio broadcast about the invasion, before it was launched.

There is a well-known conversation that Churchill had with one of his generals, the weekend before the Germans attacked Russia. During a discussion about the content of the radio broadcast, the general asked Churchill how he would treat the Soviets after they were invaded, taking into account what they had said and done to Britain since the war began. Churchill replied stating that any enemy of Germany was an ally of Britain, no matter what had gone before. If Hitler had invaded hell, Churchill stated that he would find a way to make a favorable comment about the devil.

By invading Russia before defeating Britain and changing his strategy of conquering one country at a time, Hitler effectively made the mistake that cost Germany the war. Instead of making a second attempt to invade Britain with another attempt to gain air superiority, he decided that his best option was to leave Britain to one side, strangle its supplies by the use of U-Boats, then come back and finish the job after he had dealt with the Russians. It probably seemed like a good plan at the time!

Operation Barbarossa should have been launched by mid-May 1941, however it was mid-June before the onslaught began. The delay was due to Britain unexpectedly sending fifty thousand men to help Greece defend their homeland from a combined German and Italian attack. The expanded Greek conflict temporarily caused crucial forces to divert from the Russian front. Whilst the brave Greeks were ultimately defeated, Churchill believed the months' delay was a critical factor in preventing Russia from collapsing under the German onslaught before the end of the year. The months' delay stopped the Germans reaching Moscow (and they were within thirty miles), before having to contend with the onset of a harsh Russian winter, which stopped them in their tracks. When the campaign renewed in the spring of 1942, the Russians, helped by the Allies, had regrouped and re-armed, enabling them to go on and ultimately defeat the Germans.

Churchill couldn't believe his luck when Russia was invaded, he hoped it would bring some relief for Britain, from constant German bombing and the Battle of the Atlantic, but it did nothing of the sort. For the first twelve months, it caused Britain great difficulties. The passing of the American lend-lease bill a couple of months before the attack meant Britain was finally beginning to receive vast supplies of arms from America. As they were being shipped across the Atlantic, large portions of these arms had to be diverted to Russia. Equipment earmarked for the defense of the British Empire in the Far East went instead to Russia, contributing to the ease with which the Japanese captured Hong Kong, Burma and Singapore. It was during this period that Churchill discovered how difficult it was to deal with Stalin and the Russians.

Post war analysis of German records clearly indicated that the Russians had it coming, betrayal was planned and inevitable, it was only a matter of timing. In 1941, the Russians appeared to be disappointed in the British for not losing, holding them responsible for changing the course of the war to their disadvantage. Whilst this was technically correct, what Stalin failed to realize was that if Britain had been defeated, Russia would have had no chance against the Germans. It would have just delayed the inevitable.

Rudolf Hess had flown to Scotland on his own a few months before the Russian invasion; he had been a friend of Hitler's who had lost favor since the start of the war. He hoped to regain Hitler's confidence by persuading the King of England that he was a friend and admirer of Britain, who would like to make peace. Post war records showed that Hitler did not even know about the visit, denouncing him as a traitor once the mission became public. Ever suspicious, the Russians harbored the belief that Britain had made a pact with the Germans, enabling them to invade Russia without giving them too many problems during the operation. Stalin quizzed Churchill about the Hess incident, when they met in 1944, and would not accept Churchill's emphatic denial.

Churchill worked hard to create a strong dialogue with Roosevelt, he wrote to him almost every day. He tried to get something similar going with Stalin, but he was not interested.

Communications from Stalin were always matter of fact and cold.

Churchill showed extraordinary patience and tact when dealing with Stalin especially considering the circumstances. Stalin, who would have delighted in seeing Britain under Nazi rule, now demanded that Britain give up all new American arms in their favor. Churchill related a story to illustrate his point. On a mission to Moscow two months after the attack, a Russian guide was showing around a British security guard. "That is King George railway station formerly Goering Station. This is Beaverbrook Street formerly Ribbentrop Street and that is Churchill Square formerly Hitler Square", he then asked the British soldier if he would like a cigarette, to which he replied "yes thank you comrade, formerly b*$!%&d" No matter what Britain did or the risks they took getting weapons to Russia, it was never good enough. The Russians rarely, if ever, said thank you or showed any appreciation, even when hundreds of British sailors died trying to help them.

As soon as the attack on Russia took place, Stalin insisted that Britain open up a second front by attacking Northern France. This was impossible in 1941; anyone with a rudimentary knowledge of warfare knew that it would take years before Britain could have the slightest chance of successfully invading France. The Russians did not accept any of the detailed arguments put forward by Churchill and his commanders. Regardless of how many times the facts were reiterated, they continued insisting that France should be invaded immediately, drawing troops and planes away the east, even if this meant exposing Britain to mortal peril. All this from the country that was quite content to stand back and support Germany's attempt to invade Britain. The British communists suddenly started painting the slogan "Second Front Now" across the land trying to encourage the British to invade France and draw German troops away from Russia.

Churchill tried replicating the same friendly approach that he had with Roosevelt, and failed. He concluded that the only way to deal with the Russians was to keep to the facts. No matter what arguments they put forward for their demands, he should stay resolute and firm in his dealings with them. In Stalin, he was dealing with someone who had a completely different belief system to Roosevelt, a man who believed in democracy based on western Christian values. I have no idea what belief system Stalin had. Based on Churchill's dealings with him, it appeared the only people Stalin cared about were himself and a few Russians. He had no consideration for the problems facing the British or anyone else. He would have been content to see Britain give up all available weapons to Russia and place the country at great risk, without the slightest consideration.

Once Churchill understood this, dealings with Stalin, whilst always difficult, became easier to rationalize. Churchill would ensure he did the best he could to help Russia, making decisions about them based on his own belief system. By approaching his dealings with them in this way, he avoided upset every time they treated tremendous British sacrifice without thanks or appreciation. It simply became the expected response, not something to cause annoyance. It was how Russia did business, nothing anyone could do was going to change them.

Despite his laidback approach, one incident really annoyed Churchill; Stalin sent him a letter of complaint regarding a delay in shipping equipment to Russia. The Germans were desperate to stop Britain supplying weapons to the Soviets and heavily targeted convoys on the long and dangerous journey across freezing waters to Archangel. Given the strains on the Royal Navy, it was often difficult to defend large convoys for the whole journey; as a result, the Merchant Navy suffered terrible losses regularly losing over half of a convoy. The shipments had to be suspended for a few months, in order to explore a safer means of delivery.

Churchill wrote to Stalin explaining the situation in detail; Stalin wrote a dreadfully offensive letter back to Churchill. The Russian ambassador in London delivered the letter in person. Because it had already been copied to the British ambassador in Moscow (who probably had one of the most difficult diplomatic jobs in history), Churchill knew the contents of the letter before it was delivered. When the Russian ambassador arrived, letter in hand,

Churchill refused to accept it, immediately returning the letter to the ambassador unopened. Because he did not officially read it, he did not officially have to write a reply. As a result, he did not have provide a response, which diplomatically would not have been helpful. Neither did he have to defend the British position without appearing to apologize for it. This approach left a strong impression with Stalin, confirming that Churchill would not fall for the bullying tactics that he usually employed to great effect.

The use of the phrase "belief system" is in the absence of any better description available to me. It attempts to describe the values a person adopts within a given group, section of society or culture. Not in a particularly religious way, although that might play some part, but as a way of explaining why some individuals behave differently, treat people differently, have different values and expectations than others. This can apply to different sections of the same society and to different regions of a country. Some French friends of mine would confirm that the only people the French dislike more than the English are the Parisians. They are perceived by the rest of France as being rude and ungrateful in the way they treat everyone.

This also applies to the way people behave in business. Over the years, I have worked with colleagues, managers and customers that adopt Stalin's approach to business. Additional effort put in on their behalf is taken for granted. They do not acknowledge it and simply expect more and more. The greater the help offered, the more they seek to take advantage. These type of people look at the world entirely from their own point of view, everyone else appears to exist only to be of service to them. Like Stalin, whilst their own belief system revolves entirely around themselves, they also recognize that someone with a more reasonably balanced belief system is ripe for exploitation. They are entirely comfortable manipulating people who are helpful, to their own advantage.

The trick in business, when dealing with these types of people, is to avoid letting them get under your skin. Treat the Stalin's of this world fairly and firmly, stick to the facts in any dealings with them. Whilst the Stalin's will "try it on" constantly, by demonstrating to them that they cannot manipulate the situation to their advantage, boundaries are set for the business discussion. One trick they might employ is to deliberately try and cause a person to lose their temper, believing they have the upper hand when this happens. Nothing better indicates to a Stalin that someone cannot be intimidated than when they stay calm and rational throughout an argument or heated discussion. A Stalin might well begin to shout, pretend to be angry or personally upset; these are just some of the tricks of the trade that often helps a Stalin get what they want. It is easier to remain calm and deal rationally with a Stalin when the facts are adhered to, and despite their efforts to stray into speculation, feigned emotion or upset, the discussion remains anchored to reality.

During my time at one company, my boss pulled me to one side and asked if it would be possible to add a very difficult account to my portfolio of customers. The owner of the company had been complaining to my boss about the ineffectiveness of his account manager. Just to complicate matters my business had just employed an ex member of his staff, against his wishes. At the time, they were a relatively small account. I vividly remember the first meeting we had in his boardroom. His wife who worked with him, was also present.

After the usual pleasantries, he forcefully stated that he was very annoyed with my company and that unless I could give him certain assurances regarding the access that his ex-employee had to his account information then he would be moving all his business to a competitor. He delivered this statement in a very confrontational way. I stayed calm and explained how the internal systems worked and that it was very unlikely that his ex-employee could gain access to his information. Not content with this he then demanded that I give him a cast iron guarantee that his ex employee was not able to access information, and I stated that I could not. Knowing the systems as I did, I repeated that it was very unlikely that it could happen. He then insisted that the systems were re-designed in order that he could have his guarantee. I explained that this was not possible. He then reached the peak of his anger and stated that it was not good enough; and he was going to move his business.

Whilst appearing calm on the outside but inwardly quite shaky I decided that his account was beyond salvation and no amount of re-stating or explanation was going to change the situation. I explained that I was very disappointed that I had not been able to meet his expectations and that he would have to do what he felt was best for his business. I silently began to put my things away on the basis that the meeting had concluded.

He then realized that he had pushed things further than he wanted them to go; whilst the business I worked for was not perfect, it was without doubt the best service provider compared to the competition at the time. He was aware that new products were just about to be launched, which he could profitably resell. He also realized that whilst he did not like what he was hearing, at least he had an honest answer from someone with integrity and resolve. He then offered me a coffee and asked me to talk him through some of the new products due to launch, considerably softening his tone in the process. After another hour the meeting finished on a positive note. He developed into one of the business's biggest customers and still is to this day. He is one of the great characters of the reseller community, our paths still cross, and it is always an absolute pleasure spending time with him.

The meeting demonstrated that sometimes it is possible to come across someone who appears to behave like a Stalin, but having gained their respect, they turn out to be an incredibly decent person, and a pleasure to do business with. It does not happen that often but when it does, it delivers a great sense of personal satisfaction and achievement.

With regularity, business situations arise which can be rather uncomfortable. Often a team member will need me to deliver some bad news, or an irate customer who does or does not have a valid complaint wants to bring attention to a particular issue. Instinctively some customers will be reasonable and recognize that you are doing your best in difficult circumstances, however they want to register their dissatisfaction. Others are just plain tortuous to deal with and go out of their way to be as obnoxious as possible, no matter what is said.

Whilst never looking forward to this type of meeting or conference call, over the years my ability to deal with these situations has improved. Without realizing it, this improvement has been the result of moving closer to the way Churchill handled the same type of situation; staying calm, sticking to the facts and not responding emotionally to any aggressive behavior. Since reading his memoirs, I am now even more confident that the approach I take is the best method for me to deal with tough situations.

One of the most difficult things I have experienced is when treating a Stalin the same as the vast majority of the great people who form part of daily business interaction. It is only natural to do your utmost for the decent customers and the absolute minimum for the nightmare ones. The problem is that this makes the nightmare customers worse. The trick, and it is a difficult one to master, is to try to do as much for the nightmare ones as those who are decent. By dealing with everyone equally, it makes business much more straightforward and even though satisfaction can be derived from doing the absolute minimum for the nightmare customer, in effect when this happens, they win, because in making a decent person behave in this way they have exported part of their belief system. This can only be detrimental.

It is important to treat those with a different belief system based on your own; it is easier to deal with people more effectively when working within a set of comfortable personal business boundaries. In essence, this is how Churchill managed to deal with Stalin and the rest of the unsavory characters from the war.

It is possible to expand on this topic considerably. Once an area of this kind is touched upon, dealing with behavior and beliefs, it can go on forever. This chapter is limited to my own personal experience.

It is not possible to know what Churchill's belief system was, in the context of this chapter, however, in his own words he clearly describes how he dealt with Stalin. Helping Russia to the best of his ability despite the difficulties and insults suffered as a result. By dealing with Stalin in this way, he knew that he could comfortably defend his position in the face of criticism.

Chapter 17

Entities Can't Show Loyalty

The way the British people treated Churchill after he dedicated his life to defeating the Germans beautifully illustrates the point of this chapter.

The British war government between 1940 and 1945 was a coalition of all the parties. Politics stayed subdued in parliament largely due to the desire to win. Once victory started to look inevitable, party politics became more prevalent. After Victory in Europe, it went in to overdrive. Churchill tried to persuade Clement Attlee, the opposition leader, not to press for an election until victory over Japan. It seemed wrong to hold one whilst the army was still fighting in the Far East. Victory over Japan was by no means certain and Attlee did not want to wait any longer than necessary, figuring an early election was to his benefit. Atlee, the opposition labor party leader, was entitled to ask for an election. He had concluded an agreement with Churchill to this effect some years before.

Atlee ran a brilliant campaign distinguishing between Churchill the war leader and Churchill the conservative politician. Atlee argued that the Labor party would take greater care of the returning soldiers than the conservatives would. The great Churchill historian Roy Jenkins believed he did not run a particularly effective campaign, making quite a few errors of judgment in the way he referred to the labor party. Churchill had a great weight on his mind; he was deeply troubled about Russia's plans for Europe while Britain was full of the euphoria of victory. Churchill had to keep a brave face on what he believed could be the beginnings of the cold war.

Churchill argued that his own campaign was at a major disadvantage as most of the people who ran the regional conservative party machine still hadn't returned from the war, whilst a larger part of Labor's organization was in-tact, Labor party workers largely consisting of the essential skilled people needed for the production of war materials.

None-the-less, Churchill could not believe that after everything he had done for Britain, the British public would not allow him to remain in office after the war, to help with the reconstruction. Before Churchill went off to attend the victory peace conference with the Russians and Americans in Potsdam, Britain had an election. The declaration of the result was delayed for three weeks because all soldiers' votes from around the world needed to be counted. Everyone at the conference was confident that Churchill would win, however Churchill took Attlee along in the role of observer, just in case. Before the conference was finished, Churchill and Attlee returned to Britain for the result. In one of the great election upsets of all time, Churchill lost. He never went back to Potsdam.

Clementine told Churchill, it was a blessing in disguise. He replied "at the time it was very well disguised". In reality, it probably did Churchill a favor. Whilst reading the memoirs it became clear just how much death and heartache Churchill had to endure during his five years as Prime Minister.

He related a story about how he sailed to America on the brand new battleship the Prince of Wales, shortly after Pearl Harbor. How much he enjoyed the company of the Captain, how he vividly recalled the emotional service he attended on the deck packed with the combined US and British Navy on a bright, crisp, Sunday morning. How Roosevelt and the crew sang hymns to stir the heart as they joined in the march to victory, and how three months later the captain and crew of the Prince of Wales were dead, sunk by a Japanese torpedo air attack trying to defend Singapore. The books are packed with examples of heroic figures who died for their country and the cause of freedom, many of them close friends of Churchill's. How he could cope with the remorseless pain and sorrow whilst carrying on so effectively is a mystery and one that nobody should ever have to learn by experience again.

What Churchill's books grimly illustrate is the random nature by which all these people died. Death could visit any one of them at any time. Churchill was devastated at losing the election and took a long time to get over it. He remained leader of the Conservative party and in 1951 at the age of seventy six he became leader of the country once more, staying in power for four years, running a very successful government.

As Churchill discovered, a person's value to a population or a business is limited to what they believe that person can do for them in the future, not on the achievements of the past. It never ceases to amaze me when people complain about having committed their heart and soul to a job for years, only to receive a redundancy notice without ceremony, assuming their company had a memory and would be grateful for what they did. Companies do not show loyalty, because they cannot. There is no such thing as corporate memory, or corporate feelings. Businesses do not have a heart; they exist on paper to generate money for investors and shareholders. Individuals show loyalty to one another and it is individuals that constitute a company.

Soldiers go to war for a cause but fight and make sacrifices for the people with whom they fight. They have the greatest loyalty to the men and women they train and fight with and it is these soldiers they do not want to let down in battle.

Good businesses often try to create an environment which encourages loyalty and that is a good thing. In order to create loyalty they provide employees with good services and benefits seeking to create a pleasant and rewarding working environment. Employees who feel valued and enjoy their job will be more productive.

Working for a good company can be extremely enjoyable, putting in long hours and working hard to help make something a success. This is easy to confirm from experience, having done so regularly.

No matter how hard someone works, or how good they are, for no reason they can find themselves out of a job. It just happens sometimes. They might be the most knowledgeable person with regard to a particular technology and feel completely secure in their position. The next day a rival with a similar technology acquires the company, they retain their own staff and shortly afterwards tickets to the dance are delivered in the post, "the redun-dance". It just happens.

When something like this occurs, it can have unfortunate personal side effects. A person might be flat broke living from pay-check to pay-check. It is sad, it is personal to those involved but the company will soon forget and move on.

During many years of employment no dance tickets have ever been delivered to me, although there have been a few close scrapes. At one company, the entire sales and support staff were invited to a meeting at a hotel near the office on a Monday morning. Half the group were asked to go into one room and the other half into the adjoining room. My half kept their jobs the other half had to go back to the office, collect their belongings and hand in their car keys. (To this day, I am always suspicious of large meetings in hotels). It was a few days later that I realized that my senior manager Jon, had given me a clue the Friday before the meeting. As we were leaving the office he said I had made the shortlist for the career development program he was announcing shortly, but to keep it to myself until the announcement was made public. It was very kind of him to give me such a clue, although I wasn't sharp enough to realize either at the time or on the Monday during all the stress of the moment. I've never forgotten it.

This chapter probably reads very cynically, when it should not. During twenty-seven years of continual employment, I have had no more than a week's break between leaving one job and starting the next and less than ten days sick during this long career. These are not the words of some bitter disgruntled ex employee.

The parallel of how Churchill lost the election and the way people in business are treated struck a chord and was worth sharing. It is surprising how often we complain about a company mercilessly dumping us after many years of loyal service. An old manager put it concisely when he said that redundancy was an occupational hazard. No one can expect to get through a career without it happening. He had been made redundant a few times and had learned the lesson from experience.

True loyalty as opposed to corporate loyalty tends to limit itself to the immediate group of people someone works with. The amount of loyalty reflects the way people actually treat each other. Fine words and all the right noises will make no difference when it comes to the crunch, when you really need someone's help, they will only be prepared to go the extra mile if you have shown sincere commitment to them, and gone the extra mile yourself.

Throughout a long career working for many managers, some good, some bad, some awful, one manager stands head and shoulders above the rest. I worked with him for many years across two businesses, the majority of the qualities described in this book, he demonstrated regularly. One quality which stood out above all others was his ability to command genuine loyalty from the people who worked for him. For those who were prepared to work hard and show genuine commitment he had a way of returning it, converting it into a genuine feeling of loyalty and respect. He managed to do this while setting firm boundaries. He could be decidedly ruthless and was perfectly comfortable giving out a dressing down when the occasional mistake occurred.

He had a way of controlling his temper during situations that would have me boiling over with anger. The kind of manager that made the many years working for him the best so far during my career. The reason for highlighting such a great manager is that when talking about the benefits of creating an environment based on real loyalty, it comes from actual experience. Having worked in environments that do not foster this type of loyalty my preference is clear.

To finish off I would like to relate a story from a recent holiday my wife and I took in Bermuda. We were chatting to Eileen from New York and her nephew Bill. Eileen illustrated the point of this chapter perfectly. She was a senior engineer, having worked her way up the corporate ladder for a communications company. After eighteen years, Eileen had achieved real success having put heart and soul into her job. There was a company take-over. To give an indication of the type of people who bought the company, her boss read about her redundancy in a newspaper. Two days later Eileen was out of a job. Thankfully, Eileen was able to relate this story with a smile as she was currently doing very well, working in engineering for a well-known American News Network.

It just happens!